Enterprise Risk Management

STRAIGHT TALK FOR NONPROFITS

UPLIFT FUNDING MONITOR
NOURISH PLAN NURTURE REPUTATION IMPROVE NOURISH
SHARING BOARD SUPPORT CHANGE HOUSING
CATASTROPHE CHARITABLE REPUTATION
HEALTHCARE BUDGET MANAGE CYBER EXPENSE
HOPE RESILIENCY
SERVICE VOLUNTEER LOSS HELP
THREAT INSURANCE UNCERTAINTY GRANTS
ORGANIZATION STRENGTH EDUCATE
FIX RISK STRATEGY LAWSUIT
REGULATION FOUNDATION SECURITY LEADERSHIP COMMUNITY SOCIAL MEDIA
HELP DONATE SURPRISE
WELCOME SAFETY

Al Decker   Donna Galer

Dedication

This book is dedicated to the women and men who work and volunteer in nonprofits to make the world a better place to live.

Thank you

Donna Galer and Al Decker

Table of Contents

The Last Thing You Want To Think About!

We thought we'd entitle this introductory chapter "The Last Thing You Want To Think About" because in reality, managing your risk is probably the last thing that anyone wants to think about. If you're like most nonprofits and many other organizations, there are a host of other issues that come to mind as the most important ones you need to deal with on your day-to-day walk toward keeping your nonprofit going. Funding and development are probably at the top of your list, followed closely by maintaining staff, recruiting and managing volunteers. All, of course, in support of THE most important issue – serving the needs of your constituents.

Your mission. Your vision. The people whose lives you enhance. That's the reason you started or joined the nonprofit you work so hard for. That's what is most important. Everything else exists only to help your nonprofit serve that mission and vision.

But unlike the for-profit world, where there is a product or a service that provides a source of revenue and where workers are motivated by career goals, nonprofits exist in a world with far more uncertainty.

Although some funding may be driven by clients paying something for the services you provide, the bulk of your funding is often based on donors, corporate grants, Federal, State or local government funding programs, which are subject to changes in the geopolitical climate or the good will of people or organizations, who see the benefit of your programs. At some level, even government funding boils down to goodwill in terms of the attitudes of elected officials, or perhaps at a more foundational level, the people who elect them. It is, as most organizations have learned at one point or another, a fairly uncertain world.

It is no different with your staff and complement of volunteers. Although there are some very large nonprofits that have highly paid positions and plenty of opportunity for personal advancement, the vast number of nonprofits in the world are managed and staffed by individuals who are motivated more by a passion for the cause than expectations of personal financial or career gain. Fulfilling a personal passion rather than earning a necessary living means that motivation becomes far more qualitative and essentially more uncertain in terms of staff retention.

Uncertainty is synonymous with risk. It is a state or environment which involves imperfect, unknown or sometimes unpredictable information. A world where many factors are outside of an individual's or organization's control. Sure, the for-profit world must deal with many uncertainties. But for nonprofits, uncertainty touches more aspects of their operations and is an everyday fact of life. Quite simply, it's a world full of risk. And risk, like every other aspect of your organization, is something that can and should be managed.

Some of the risks may be easy to identify, e.g. funding risk:

- the loss of a significant portion of funding,

- a large donor finds another worthy cause,

- a government program contains a sunset clause which a new administration no longer finds a priority,

- a failing economy that simply puts a strain on contributions from all sources, government and non-government alike.

Then there is key person risk. The success of your organization is likely due in large part to the passion of the founder, the Executive Director and key staff. In other words, people who, if the organization loses, could have a significant impact on the continued success of the organization.

These are the easy ones to identify. But how about the subtler risks? What about issues like your reputation, attitudes toward your services, the never-ending stream of technology changes, staff who operate in silos, time constraints, being spread too thin, poor governance, or security concerns around key documents/business information or other critical information that reside on personal laptops or is kept in people's heads? The list can go on and on. The most critical point to consider, and the good news is, that these risks can be managed. Can they all be eliminated? No. Can you think of every last risk? No.

So, what can you do about it?

You may not be able to think of everything, but you can identify a lot of your risks and you can prepare for most of them, even if that preparation is no more than being aware of the potential for that risk to occur. Louis Pasteur once said, "chance favors the prepared". Or said another way, if things change, you are better able to handle the change or possibly take advantage of the change, if you had previously thought about it and considered what you might do should such an event occurred. Being surprised is rarely a good thing and, even if there is little or nothing you can do about something, having a plan for what you might do is far better than reacting to the situation only after it occurs. This book will try to show you how to deal with and more effectively manage your risk.

The purpose of this book is simple — **it is to give you more confidence that you have reduced the uncertainty in your plan** by 1) understanding the importance of managing the risk that exists within the uncertain nonprofit environment, 2) making you more effective in dealing with that risk, and 3) helping you to ensure that you are successful in carrying out the mission and vision of your organization.

Managing your risk is more than buying insurance, having a business continuity or disaster recovery plan or complying with regulations. It's thinking through each risk. If the risk occurs, how will it affect my plans? Can I modify some process or condition to minimize the possibility of the risk occurring? Can I manage around it? Should I alter plans so as to avoid it?

The prospect of managing risk can seem overwhelming. Just a glance at some of the international standards for Enterprise Risk Management (ERM) could make anyone think it is just too much to deal with. We hope to change that view with this book. We believe the entire process can be boiled down into five very manageable steps that can be sized or scaled to fit your organization's needs. In addition to other topics we believe are important to the overall process, we will discuss how to 1) identify, 2) prioritize, 3) mitigate, 4) monitor and 5) report on risk.

Chapter 1

Nonprofit Risk Landscape

Is there more risk in the world today than there was just twenty years ago? Most people would say yes in answer to that question. Some of the heightened risk level comes in the form of:

- Cyber Crime

- Technological Advances/Obsolescence

- Climate Change

- Terrorism

- Socio-economic Volatility

- Increased Regulation and Reporting Requirements

Nonprofits are not immune to any of these. In fact, some of these risk areas are more dangerous for nonprofits which typically do not have the resources to respond to them. For example, the kind of technology protection needed to prevent or respond to a successful cyber hacking may be beyond the financial or expertise capabilities of many nonprofits.

Nonprofits face a plethora of internal risks at the same time that external risks are escalating. And some of these internal ones are exacerbated by external factors such as the ones above, as well as others.

Among some of the not so new but potentially lethal internal risks that nonprofits face are:

- Insufficient Fiscal Oversight
- Poor Control Environment
- Lack of Proper or Sufficient Talent
- Lack of Succession Planning
- Ineffective Board Governance
- Donor Mishandling

Fiscal Oversight/Control Environment

When the 110-year-old YWCA of Southeast Raleigh, NC closed its doors in 2012 due to financial issues, it was shock to just about everyone, reportedly including the staff and Board. The risk of financial instability was not recognized. Why? There have been numerous articles written about this organization's closure which discuss some of the details behind what happened.[1]. Simply put, at the most fundamental level, the risk was not fully identified or vetted and effective mitigation was not implemented. In a risk aware culture, would this have happened? Probably not.

Governance

Several high-profile firings of nonprofit executive directors show how quickly a private, internal matter can explode into a very public debacle that absorbs resources and causes reputational harm. These dismissals came at the Aspen Film Festival [2]., Huntsman Cancer Institute [3]. and Oklahoma's Feed The Children [4]. organization. Regardless of the merits of these respective firings (one of which has been over-turned with good reason as of this writing), it should be asked whether the risks associated with the termination decision were clearly identified, were mitigation actions taken in advance of the action and would the decision to terminate have been the same, if the risks were thought out.

The point is that even something which would seem to be within the purview, scope and right of boards to do can evoke significant risk of expensive legal suits, reputation damage and time diverted from the organization's mission.

When a risk materializes and becomes an event, the reverberations may be felt forever. They may take the form of an immediate existential threat such as the closure of the nonprofit or they may take the form of a never-ending diminishment of the nonprofit's potential.

The risk of inadequate governance and fraud are very real in the nonprofit sphere where people who want to do good have a hard time imagining that others may consciously engage in wrong doing. Readers may remember or can read about the 1992 resignation and subsequent conviction of The United Way's National President, William V. Aramony, for fraud and tax evasion.

According to a New York Times article written by David Cay Johnston. "Five years after its former national president was found to be converting charity money to his own use, United Way is in crisis, abandoned by 4.5 million people -- 20 percent of its donors. And most of its 17.7 million remaining donors give less through payroll deduction, United Way's bread and butter."

"If donations had continued to rise as fast as they did in the five years before the scandal, United Way would have raised $4.14 billion last year. Instead it raised $3.25 billion, down 11 percent from 1991 but up slightly from 1995. (All figures are adjusted for inflation.)" [5].

Fast forward to 2016, based on information in Forbes, the revenue for the United Way for the fiscal year ending June 30, 2016 was $3.87 billion.[6]. Readers can draw their own conclusion about the potential for long-lasting repercussions from a risk that was not sufficiently identified or mitigated.

Organizations which recognize the very real threat of fraud and deal with it as a key risk that must be identified, monitored, reduced, and reported, if found, will be on much more solid ground long term.

Abraham Nicholas Garza did not expect to die when he showed up for work at a California based Goodwill site. Unfortunately, he was crushed to death in a loading dock incident. Also unfortunate is that this might have been avoided. As reported in a Sacramento newspaper, "Serious and willful safety violations by Goodwill in Sacramento led to the grisly death last year of a 26-year-old loading dock worker at one of its outlet stores, say state regulators who issued six citations and more than $100,000 in fines against the giant nonprofit."[7]. Goodwill proceeded to blame the driver of the equipment which backed into Mr. Garza and to fire him. However, it turns out that this operator's personnel file shows he had written numerous letters to Goodwill's management about safety issues at this location long before the accident took place.[8] The risks surrounding heavy machinery are clear the need for safety guidelines and training is obvious and undisputable. So, why were they ignored at this Goodwill site? Without knowing the answer, it can, at minimum, be hypothesized that managing risk was not a priority. And in this case, the greatest loss was measured in human life.

These examples are extreme. Day after day, nonprofits are besieged by risks with varying degrees of potential impact. We have alluded to some in the Introduction and earlier in this chapter. The loss of a major donor, a downturn in the local or national economy, a competitor agency which takes some of the government funding that might have gone to yours, a building that is declared unsafe for use by government inspectors, a client who sues for some reason, these all start out as risk which needs to be identified and mitigated before it materializes. Not every risk can be recognized and not all risks should be mitigated. Some risks are too hard to recognize and some are too insignificant or remote to merit mitigation. However, every major risk that is knowable should be identified and addressed.

The risk landscape for nonprofits is rocky and littered with quicksand and fissures. A nonprofit that fails to undertake appropriate and reasonable risk management will not get 'a pass' by the public or regulators. To navigate across this landscape requires more than what may be the current way of doing things. These examples show why a dedicated, delineated yet integrated process for identifying and addressing risks is so necessary and important. In a later chapter, a risk management process will be detailed.

Chapter 2

Black Swans, Grey Swans

By now we should all be familiar with the term "black swan". They are typically characterized as a highly improbable events with devastating consequences that no one saw coming. After the fact, the event does not look so improbable and everyone knows exactly what should have been done to prevent the event or at least minimize the impact of the event. Many black swan events are created by a multiplicity of risks converging, also termed a "perfect storm". But even a single large and unanticipated risk can create many losses and issues through-out an enterprise whether the enterprise is a corporation, association, nation state or region. It's easy to become the Monday morning quarterback for such unexpected events, but what about events we all saw coming, yet still wound up being caught by surprise.

Although black swans certainly can and will have a significant impact on nonprofits, they are to a large degree, events that are outside of our control. We believe nonprofits are far more susceptible to a slightly different shade of swan

– the Grey Swan. As a matter of fact, they may be the single greatest type of risk to nonprofits overall.

Grey swans can have all the devastating impact of a black swan on a nonprofit. The major difference is that whereas a black swan is completely unexpected, a grey swan is something we probably saw coming, but for some reason, never got around to doing anything about until it actually occurs. Chapter 2, describes some common threads for failures at nonprofits. But in addition to the commonality of these types of events, there is another common factor that allows these common events to be the downfall of a nonprofit and that is - everything is great till everything is falling apart.

- A senior Executive Director retires or suddenly passes away.
    › Maybe there should have been a succession plan in place
- 25% of the organization's funding from a government source is lost due to changes in the geopolitical atmosphere
    › Maybe there should have been more thought about politics and either a plan developed of what steps could be taken should the funds be lost or consideration given to setting aside more funds as a cushion to provide time to adjust.

The shuttering of a 110-year-old YMCA was not likely caused by one single catastrophic event but by the culmination of many smaller ones that someone within the organization should have noticed long before it resulted in the closing of the nonprofit.

How many board meetings have you attended where everything is going along just fine? And then boom – the floor falls out.

That the virtually unpredictable can and does occur is well documented. Despite sophisticated quantitative models and worst-case scenario planning, unexpected, previously unimaginable events do occur. Even more frequent are events that seem unlikely but for which there have been incremental steps or signs to signal their possibility. Of course, there are times when the unpredictable can be a positive. But from the standpoint of protecting an organization from negative consequences, Enterprise Risk Management is designed to ensure that the organization's models and worst-case scenarios are considered in order to make the unpredictable more predictable.

So, what are the characteristics of a grey swan? Unlike a black swan which almost no one would ever have thought could happen, grey swans are much more predictable. We know they could happen. They hide in plain sight. They are the elephant in the room that we avoid talking about. They are masked by enthusiasm for the mission of the organization and the hope that something will happen to fix the problem.

They can beget other risks similar to setting up a line of dominos, one falls and the rest come tumbling down. Or they can be part of correlated risks such that when one happens then others happen at the same time.

A very recent real-life example of a grey swan is the Tax Cuts and Jobs Act of 2018. Tax Reform was the subject of the presidential race of 2016. When President Trump's administration started working on what would become the Act referenced above, no one knew the final form it would take. Up until the last minute there was a scramble to fine tune many provisions in the bill. Having said that, the nonprofit world could see there was risk in the reform depending how personal deductions were to be treated. There was always potential for negative consequences for nonprofits. In fact, the risk was real and the negative consequences are estimated to be quite significant.

As reported in The Economist, "By doubling the standard deduction, estimates are that between 90-95 percent of filers will not itemize their returns, thus walling off the charitable deduction from all but 5-10 percent of filers. The Tax Policy Center estimates this change will reduce charitable giving by up to $20 billion a year."[1]

The nonprofit world has to ask itself to what extent it saw the grey swan, to what degree did it act to avoid the risk through lobbying and communicating and how much it did to mitigate the risk by augmenting its capital base in advance. We can hope that something positive does come out of this situation in terms of some donors becoming more generous to overcome generally reduced giving or in terms of nonprofits becoming even better at fund raising and financial management.

In summary, for the most part, we actually do know when a grey swan risk exists but, either don't believe it's necessary to do something about it or let inertia take over so we put off action till it's too late.

Do we just keep making excuses as to why we're not taking any action, such as:

- The solution would be too costly
- There are too many things on our collective plates already.
- A dismissal stated as: "all nonprofits have the same problems" or "we've suffered through situations like this before and we are still around. We'll be able to handle anything else that comes up."
- There were more important matters to worry about.

So, what should an organization do? As we will discuss in the chapter on developing an ERM process, the very first step is to identify your risks, including gray swans! Document all the risk issues you probably already know about. If you document the risks, you are more likely to begin to think about how you can mitigate them. And if you build on the existing list of risks as new ones are recognized, it is more likely that you will maintain a sound risk awareness at all times.

Chapter 3

Need For Robust Risk Management

In the previous chapters we started building the case for why nonprofits need to take risk management seriously. Given the risk landscape, it behooves founders, boards, and executive directors to deal with the uncertainties facing their organization in a deliberate and prudent manner.

What would such a manner entail? It means more than buying insurance or worrying about something bad happening. Essentially, it would mean identifying and addressing all major risks to the organization, both insurable and non-insurable. Later, we will go into an in-depth definition and explanation of the enterprise risk management (ERM) process which is a holistic approach to risk management which deals with all types of risks. In this chapter, we will add to the reasons why more robust risk management is needed for nonprofits.

Recognize the existance and magnitude of risk

Understand the need for managing risk

Implement a risk management process

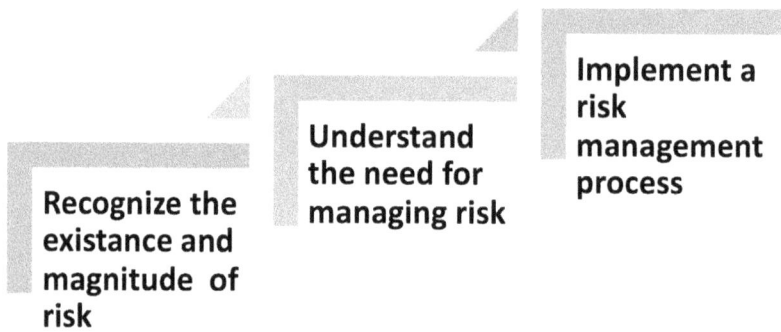

Why Insurance Is Not Enough

When an organization buys insurance, it is transferring the risk, or more precisely, it is passing off the loss associated with the risk, from themselves to the insurer. For this, they pay a premium. There may be deductibles or self-retention levels involved in structuring the insurance. Nevertheless, the transaction is a transfer of risk.

Insurers do not accept all types of risk though they are getting increasingly innovative and comprehensive in terms of what they will cover. Still, most insurances will likely never insure some types of risks, for example: 1) the risk of not adjusting the organization's strategy when social, demographic, economic changes threaten to make the current strategy or vision untenable, 2) the risk of reputational damage due to illegal or unethical actions, 3) the risk of losing funding due to any number of causes, 4) the risk of not finding the human resources (board, volunteer, etc.) needed to keep the organization running.

Insurable	Non-Insurable
Property/ Casualty Risks	Many Strategic Risks
Workers Compensation	Most Performance Risks
Life & Health	Malfeasence

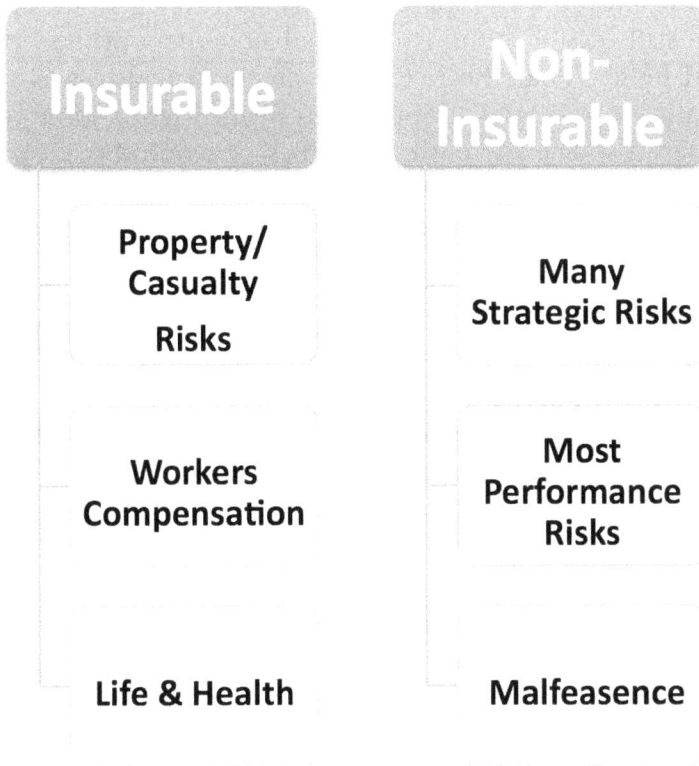

Aligning Organization Response With The Risk Landscape

In order to ensure the sustainability of the organization, both the board and staff must be risk aware. Again, this means that all significant risks must get addressed in some way. In the cases where insurance is not an option, it is still incumbent upon the leaders to take prudent action to address such risks through risk management.

Strategic Risks

Strategic risks are one of the top causes of failures in the for-profit world. Consider a nonprofit adoption agency that can no longer find an equal number of potential adoptees as there are adoptive parents thus had to close its doors while still owing reimbursements to clients who had paid initial fees.[1] What the nonprofit failed to realize was that the ratio of potential adoptees was declining for some time compared to the increasing number of would-be adoptive parents. They did not see or respond to the risk of relevant societal changes but rather continued to do business as usual.

What this situation demanded was robust risk management. An organization in the same circumstances as the one referenced should have a repeatable process in place that identified, prioritized, mitigated, and/or transferred risks and reported on them to relevant stakeholders. Such an approach would provide an early recognition of the emerging risk. Then, mitigation actions could have been implemented such as: 1) reduce the number of clients served to better match the more limited number of adoptees with a concomitant reduction in its operating expenses, 2) develop new, potentially international connections to source adoptees, 3) merge with another nonprofit adoption agency to gain synergies and become more visible to potential biological parents who are seeking adoption agencies.

Performance Risks

Consider a hypothetical nonprofit established to help other nonprofits work together in a certain locale. What if there is already another organization in that locale which is already doing bits and pieces of what the new nonprofit sees as its mission. What if there is a very slow start to setting a strategy and developing initiatives. What if the first initiative is unsuccessful because the person accountable did not have either the time or the skill to apply to the endeavor. Such an organization will likely fail. However, if it had done a robust risk assessment as part of its founding, it could have identified the risks that would lead to failure in time to make changes or abort. Frequently, when someone on the board wants to take a realistic look at the risks in front of their organization, this is diagnosed as negativity or lack of enthusiasm rather than an honest attempt to face the very real threats and uncertainties which exist. However, in reality, if risks are addressed early, they can often be minimized or overcome. At worst, an organization can prepare a respectable retrenchment or closure in response to risks which cannot be ameliorated, transferred, or avoided. Boards must be willing to participate in candid risk identification and mitigation.

Malfeasance Risks

Every organization relies on humans to perform the various roles that allow it to operate. Humans are complex beings and it is not possible (yet) to know what is going on in someone else's mind. For that reason, it is impossible to know what truly motivates a specific individual or what actions they are capable of.

Nonprofits are filled with people who want to do good for the community. They are motivated by being able to see that someone was helped, some wrong was righted or some community was improved. They are generous and give in terms of time, talent, and treasure. And they tend to think that the others involved in their organization is the same as they are. Not so. Every so often there will be those who take advantage of their position in a nonprofit for their own gain. And herein lies the risk of malfeasance.

Previously, we discussed what happened at the United Way in the 1980s. Instead of going into a laundry list of similar examples, we will simply posit that nonprofits are not immune to such a risk and may even be prone to such a risk. Therefore, risk management must be rigorously applied to identify and mitigate the nexus points that might allow that risk to materialize.

When malfeasance occurs, it can damage the organization in so many ways: 1) tarnishing reputation, 2) turning off donors, 3) demoralizing staff and volunteers, 4) creating added expense such as fines and legal costs. Bottom-line, it can be the end of the line for the organization.

What Conclusion Can Be Drawn

Despite the fact that nonprofits have existed for centuries without a lot of risk management, it should be clear that today's dynamic and danger filled environment makes it much more difficult to survive without it. Thus, regardless of the limited resources which the organization might have at its disposal, time spent on risk management is more than worth the investment.

Chapter 4

Defining ERM within your organization – Establishing the Rationale and Context

The primary purpose of any Enterprise Risk Management (ERM) program is to help an organization anticipate risks that could hinder the achievement of or alter the nature of expected outcomes or plans. In short, it is a management process that helps an organization respond to situations that may occur and that might limit its ability to achieve its strategic goals and objectives.

First and foremost, it is important to remember that ERM is a process and not a one-time activity. It is not meant to simply identify risks at a point in time, but to help the organization identify and manage risks throughout the year. In keeping with this concept, ERM is a systemic process designed to enable the organization to recognize and manage its risk on a continuous basis throughout the execution of its plan.

Definition and Purpose

All nonprofit organizations exist to achieve their specific mission and vision. ERM is a business process that, like all other operational processes, is not an end unto itself, but a means to enable the organization to meet its goals as set forth in the organization's strategic plan.

In simple terms, ERM is no more than thinking about all the things that could prevent an organization from achieving the outcomes it expects, but doing it in a formal, rigorous manner, and documenting the results. If you identify a risk, think about what you could do to either eliminate that risk or soften its blow should it occur, and write your thoughts down, you will be in a much better position to deal with that risk than if it catches you by surprise, or you try to deal with that bridge when you come to it.

ERM is simply being prepared.

There are a number of highly sophisticated and complex international guidelines that have been established that describe all that might be considered in how to establish and ERM process, but for the most part, these standards boil down to:

1. Identifying risks;

2. Prioritizing risks based on how significant they are;

3. Developing a plan to deal with those risks;

4. Monitoring those risks; and

5. Repeating the process

In essence, it is no more than good business management.

Establish the Context

More important than any "general" definition of ERM, it's important to define what ERM means to "your" organization. To do that, you need to establish the context or rationale for an ERM process as it applies specifically to your organization.

Simply start by asking yourself a question -

"What are we trying to accomplish by integrating risk management into our operations?"

Establishing the context is an essential first step to ensure an effective risk management process. Context setting needs to take into account the internal and external environment that the organization operates within, including the organization's goals, objectives, values, culture, governance, responsibilities, structure, operations, standards, guidelines, processes, systems, functions, information flow, decision making process, projects, services, assets and specific practices employed.

In simpler terms, by establishing the organizational context, the organization is able to:

1. Articulate its objectives;

2. Define the external & internal parameters to be considered when managing risk;

3. Set the scope and risk criteria within the defined risk policy; and

4. Establish a framework within which your risks are managed.

Establishing the context sets the framework within which the risk assessment should be undertaken, ensures the reasons for carrying out the risk assessment are clearly known, and provides the backdrop of circumstances against which risks can be identified and assessed.

Establish the External Context

The external context describes the environment within which the organization exists. It may include but is not limited to:

- Legal/regulatory requirements,

- Donor perceptions and expectations,

- Social, cultural, or competitive factors.

- Prevailing attitudes that may impact the organizations objectives;

- Stakeholders perception of the organizations value

External context questions to consider:

To develop the external context, the following questions might include but not be limited to:

1. What are the major external uncertainties facing the organization?

2. What plans does the organization have for responding to crises?

3. What is the public/client perception of the organization?

4. What are the aims and objectives of your organization?

5. Who is involved with your organization - both internally and externally?

6. What facilities do you have and/or use?

7. What community and donor relationships does your organization have and how important are these?

8. What laws, regulations, rules or standards apply to your organization?

9. Does your organization hold itself to a high standard of conduct?

10. Are volunteers required to have a high level of expertise?

11. What other factors are affecting your volunteer workforce?

12. Does your organization accept its responsibility for "duty of care"?

Establish the Internal Context

To establish the internal context, it is necessary to consider the organization's internal environment. This may include, but is not limited to:

- the governance model;
- organizational roles and responsibilities;
- goals, objectives, and the strategies;
- relationships with and perceptions of volunteers and staff;
- culture;
- decision-making processes (both formal and informal);

To develop the internal context, the following questions might include but not be limited to:

1. What does 'risk' mean in this organization?

2. What is the commitment of the organization to ERM?

3. What are the organization's ethical values?

4. Does the board have sufficient knowledge and experience to oversee risk?

5. Who is responsible for managing risks?

6. What has the organization learned from its experiences with risk?

7. What is your organization currently doing to manage risk, either formally or informally?

Rationale

The result of this process is to develop a clear understanding of the context within which the result of the risk analysis will be considered and the rationale for undertaking an ERM process to begin with. The rationale should help the organization to focus its effort by identifying which risks are important enough to consider, the priority of those risks within the established context and the extent to which those risks are mitigated. Quite literally the ERM rationale becomes the foundation for all subsequent work on the ERM process as a whole.

An example of a nonprofit context and rationale statement can be found in Appendix 1.

Chapter 5

It All Begins With The Strategy/Mission

It stands to reason that because ERM is intended to enable the organization to meet its strategic goals and objectives and to strengthen its sustainability, the ERM process has to begin with a thorough understanding of strategy. In the next chapter, we describe the actual process steps. But first, some discussion of strategy is in order.

Large nonprofits, like large for-profit businesses, have strategic plans that lay out the long-term: 1) vision, 2) mission, 3) values, 4) customer value proposition, 5) SWOT (strengths, weaknesses, opportunities, and threats to the organization), 6) goals and objectives, 7) tactics and transformational projects. Unfortunately, mid to small size nonprofits do not always have fully formed strategic plans and may not even have clear goals and objectives.

Strategic Plan Elements

Foundation	Targets	How To
Vision	Goals (Qualitative Targets)	Strategic Tactics
Mission		
Values	Objectives (Quantitative Targets)	
Customer Value Proposition		Transformational Projects/Initiatives
SWOT Analysis	Strategy Map (Timeline)	

Benefits of a Strategic Plan

We strongly recommend that all nonprofits take the time to develop a basic strategic plan. The benefits of having a formal strategy are:

- creates a clear picture of what the organization is/ does and is not/does not do

- sets a direction for the organization's future – rather than letting random events create the future

- provides a singular source of information that can be used (in part or in whole) to inform clients, donors, staff, volunteers, and the general public about the organization

- serves as a point of reference for decision-making and prioritizing

- acts as a catalyst for action.

Strategic Risk Exists Whether There Is A Strategy Or Not

Whether nonprofit has a documented strategy or not, it has a mission, and it has risks. The mission is whatever its purpose is, e.g. feeding the poor, advocating for the arts, collecting money for healthcare research. The risks it faces need to be addressed if the organization is to continue in its mission most effectively. It should be remembered that some risks are existential threats.

Unaddressed risk can create loss but risk that is addressed can be avoided, minimized, or even turned into opportunity.

Strategic Risks

So, what is a strategic risk? Here are some ways to think about strategic risk as opposed to operational or other types of risk. It can be anything that creates uncertainty around the ability of the organization to continue its mission. It is often caused by a change in the environment in which the organization conducts its mission but it can also be caused by internal issues. It is a risk that strikes at one of the fundamental elements of the organization. With these thoughts in mind, the following are some categories of strategic risk:

- Client Related – e.g. the client population wants or needs a different service than what is provided

- Competition Related – e.g. new entrants among nonprofits or for-profits offer the same or better services, creating competition that affects sustainability

- Reputation Related – e.g. some publicly noted crisis or scandal rocks the organization

- Donor Related – e.g. some factor, or combination of factors, causes donors to reduce or stop giving

The March of Dimes is a good example of how a risk was turned into an opportunity. In this case, the risk was a very benign and wonderful one. This story is told on the March of Dimes website.[1] The organization was founded to help find the cure for polio and to help those afflicted with the disease. There was always uncertainty around the continued need for the organization if a cure was found. And Jonas Salk did create an immunization for polio which virtually eradicated it. This could have been the end of the March of Dimes. That might have been a good end, except for the fact that all the infrastructure, donor lists, name recognition would all be dismantled amounting to a waste of what was already there. Luckily, the organization's leadership understood the risk and was following the developments pertaining to the cure. They developed a new strategy and mission for the organization. It put its significant resources toward fighting birth defects of all types!

ERM Starts With The Strategy

When we say it all begins with the strategy, what we mean is that risk identification should first focus on the risks that affect the organization's ability to meet its strategy and long-term goals and objectives. A nonprofit that lacks a strategy can find proxies for it, such as: 1) the mission, 2) the annual budget, 3) the fundraising objective, 4) the expanded service goal or building upgrade plan. The questions to ask are relatively simple:

- What clear, potential threats to our strategy exist?

- What uncertainties do we face given our particular strategy?

What dynamics are creating emerging risks that could impact our strategy or goals by the end of the strategic planning period?

Below is a template for recording strategic risks:

Strategic Element/ Goal	Risk/Uncertainty	Impact/Likelihood
Expand into additional counties	Resource scalability to orchestrate expansion	High/High
Maintain or increase funding levels despite limited donor base	Donor fatigue	High/Medium
Gain more recognition in general community	A performance issue or personal indiscretion becomes widely known and damages reputation	Medium/Low

Organizations should identify risks that are both generic (could happen to any organization such as theirs) as well as specific (could likely happen to them because of peculiarities of their organization).

Moving Ahead

It is far easier to suggest that something should be done than it is to actually do it. In the next chapters, we will go into more depth about what and how an organization can implement a robust ERM program.

Chapter 6

ERM Framework for Nonprofits

An ERM framework can be thought of as the architectural blueprint for how enterprise risk management will be structured in the organization. The structure should be an enabler. The elements of the framework include such items as: 1) the mandate for ERM, 2) who is responsible for what aspect of ERM, 3) what process will be used to do it.

On the following page is a schematic representing what an ERM framework includes:

Governance	Roles, Responsibilities & Reporting Lines	Process
ERM Board Mandate	Board	Methods for Identifying Risk
	Management	Methods for Quantifying Risks
ERM Objectives	Risk Officer	
	Risk Committee	Approaches for Mitigating Risks
ERM Control Environment	Risk Owners	Reporting Forms and Timelines

In the nonprofit world, there may not be a risk officer or a risk committee per se. In some very small nonprofits, the Board may have to handle all these elements. The point here is that the term ERM framework is commonly used and it is good to know what it refers to. The framework itself is a tool to ensure that there is thought given to each of these component parts and that each is addressed in some way or another.

Governance: Board ERM Mandate

The board mandate can be very simply stated, for example

- XYZ organization will maintain an enterprise risk management process so that risks are appropriately addressed thus enabling the achievement of the strategy and goals.

- The organization will set a risk appetite and may also set tolerances and limits.

- The board will approve the ERM framework and review periodic reports about the organization's risks.

This mandate is vitally important because it serves notice to everyone in the organization, including the Executive Director/CEO that ERM is not optional. It is common knowledge that support from the very top is critical for introducing and sustaining efforts that are new or that require resource – time, attention, etc.

Governance: ERM Objectives

Just as any business function or process has objectives to drive performance and allow for assessment of effectiveness, ERM needs objectives as well. These may be a mix of quantitative and qualitative measures. To the extent that the objectives are quantitative, this will provide greater objectivity.

Objectives are simply a way to state what is expected from someone or something. Below is a sample set of objectives for ERM which can be further enhanced as the process becomes more mature within an organization. For example, the objective to reduce the total cost of risk for the organization might become even more refined, e.g. reduce the total cost of risk by 10%.

Objectives:

- Maintain and regularly update a register of prioritized risks with mitigation plans

- Minimize surprises brought to the Board

- Reduce the cost of risk to the organization

- Reduce the number of suits brought against the organization

- Reduce the number of accidents/injuries on organization's premises

- Increase the risk awareness of staff and volunteers to minimize loss due to risk

Total cost of risk includes such items as:

1. Insurance premiums

2. Paid deductibles

3. Out of pocket legal fees due to suits or settlements, etc.

4. Fines and penalties due to non-compliance

5. Lost time due to staff or volunteer injuries sustained at work

6. Loss in revenues or funding due to a risk event

Governance: ERM Performance Review

When it comes to determining how well ERM has performed for the organization's benefit, this can be accomplished by looking at outcomes versus the objectives that have been set. For small organizations, the performance review is nothing more than that.

Larger organizations need to be aware of a construct called, "the three lines of defense". It refers to the three areas which are responsible for overseeing the effectiveness of ERM.

Three Lines of Defense

- Managers Designated as Risk Owners **"Owns and Manages Risk"**

- Risk Committees, Compliance and Legal Functions **"Oversees Risk"**

- Internal and External Audit **"Independent Assurance"**

By making sure the three lines of defense are in play help to ensure ERM is being executed as it should be. However, there still needs to be a reckoning between the objectives set versus actual results.

Roles, Responsibilities, and Reporting Lines: Board

The role of the board relative to ERM is to: 1) establish a mandate for ERM, 2) ensure that there is a process to address organization-wide risk, 3) stay apprised of significant risks to the organization and ensure execution of the actions being taken to address such risks, 4) provide input on risks, as needed.

Roles, Responsibilities, and Reporting Lines: Management

The Executive Director, CEO or topmost leader needs to strongly endorse ERM and provide the necessary resources for it to be accomplished. Staff needs to support ERM as they would any other important work of the organization.

A key way in which the Executive Director or CEO can signal the importance of ERM is by using risk information in every day communication and decision-making.

Roles, Responsibilities, and Reporting Lines: Risk Officer

Regardless of the title of person who is designated as the person who will lead the ERM process, that person's role is to manage the implementation of the steps of the process. In very small organizations, this may be the Executive Director/CEO or Finance Officer. If it is a stand-alone position it must report high enough in the organization such that it can have easy access to the Executive Director/ CEO.

Among the primary responsibilities of the risk officer are:

1. Develop the ERM framework

2. Implement the ERM process – all steps

3. Lead meetings on risk/non-Board level risk committee meetings

4. Document all findings

5. Prepare formal, routine reports for management and the Board

6. Research and communicate about current risks, emerging risks, risk management techniques

7. May manage the insurance program or this may be the role of an administrative person

8. May implement safety program or this may be the role of an administrative person or agent/broker

The risk officer may use and would need to supervise any internal or external resources to accomplish these responsibilities.

Roles, Responsibilities, and Reporting Lines: Risk Committee

If the organization is large enough to need or allow for a non-Board level risk committee, the role of the risk committee is to:

1. Support the risk officer in identifying risk, creating mitigation plans, appointing on risk owners

2. Making recommendations on how the overall process of identifying, mitigating, and reporting on risk can be improved

3. Reviewing risk reports before these are submitted to the Executive Director/CEO or Board

4. Advocating for ERM and the use of risk information in decision-making

Members of the risk committee typically include the heads of major functions such as: finance, human resources, operations, legal, marketing, etc.

Roles, Responsibilities, and Reporting Lines: Risk Owners

Risk owners are the individuals who are most likely the ones who have identified and prioritized a risk (though risks can be identified by the Board, ED/CEO, Risk Officer, Risk Committee, or anyone at any level in the organization) and are directly responsible for designing and executing the mitigation plan for risks assigned to them. Typically, that means a finance risk is assigned to the Chief Financial Officer or Treasurer, a volunteer risk is assigned to the Director of Volunteers or Volunteer Coordinator and so on.

In addition to their normal reporting line, risk owners have a dotted line to the Risk Officer or equivalent and the Risk Committee, if there is one.

The ERM Process

The ERM framework should describe how the process of identifying, quantifying and prioritizing, mitigating, and reporting risks is done in a particular organization. As will be described in the next chapter, there are various ways to do each of these process steps. For example, identifying risks can be done through e-questionnaires, live workshops, phone or website hotlines. These methods may involve all staff or only some levels of staff. They may be done annually, semi-annually, or randomly. Such details will be spelled out in the process part of the framework.

Chapter 7

The ERM Process for Nonprofits

Let us begin by reinforcing an important point. The key word in the term "Enterprise Risk Management" is management. Just like every other activity in managing an organization, it is not something that is done just once, at some arbitrary point in time. It is something that is done all the time. Risk is with us all the time. And although it is not something that should impede us by constantly worrying about it, it is something we should be constantly aware of, so that we can act appropriately, as the signs of impending risk start to surface.

The process is something that involves everyone in an organization. Even in large nonprofits that may have a person or a team of people who focus on ERM, it is still something that everyone, from the Executive Director and Board, to the staff and volunteers should be a part of. In very small organizations that could be a few as 2 or 3 people. Just because an organization is small, or of limited funds, its risks could be as real and as devastating as those for much larger organizations. We will discuss roles and responsibilities a bit later, but first we will describe the entire ERM process.

There are two primary international standards that prescribe an ERM process, ISO 31000, and COSO ERM. There are also proprietary ERM processes that organizations follow that have a great deal in common with the well-known ones mentioned. What's important is that these standards exist and represent best practices for managing risk. Approaches to ERM may vary to some degree in elements and complexity, there are five key points of the ERM process that are elemental. These five process points are:

1. Identifying risks

2. Prioritizing risks

3. Mitigating risks

4. Reporting on risk

5. Measure progress on mitigation plans

| Identify | Prioritize | Mitigate | Report | Measure |

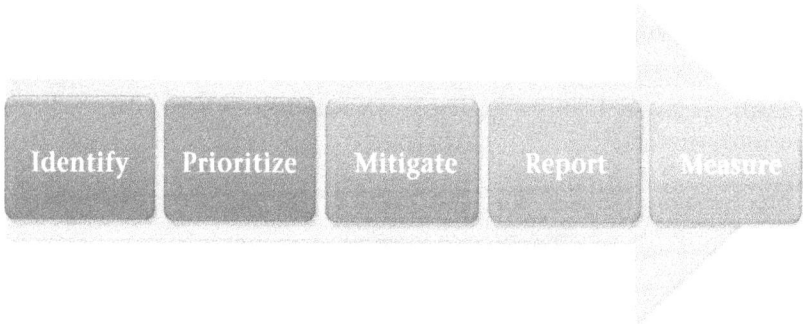

Remember, the intended purpose of engaging in ERM is to ensure that the goals and objectives of the organizations mission and vision are achieved. Managing risk doesn't always mean eliminating all risk, it is simply being prepared and not being caught by surprise.

ERM Process Point 1: Identify

Identify

There are two important considerations that come into play when identifying risk. The first is to establish a context within which the risk exists. There is no sense in considering risk that is not important to the organization or that may not significantly impact the organization's goals or strategies.

The second important consideration is that everyone in the organization needs to be involved in risk identification to some extent. No single person within an organization can possibly know all the potential risks. Thus, the more people within the organization who are risk aware, the greater the chance that significant risks will get recognized.

There are many ways to go about identifying potential risk. Many organizations begin with a broad-based risk assessment and try to consider all the possible risks the organization might be facing. Although this sounds like a good place to start, unfortunately this approach can drag the process out considerably. Delay can result in loss of momentum and interest, and usually results in identifying more risks than the organization could possible handle such as insignificant risks that may have little or no impact at all.

The best place to start is to focus your efforts on risks that are most likely to affect the primary elements of the mission and vision of the organization. There is an old expression that goes something like "What does that have to do with the price of tea in China?". In terms of ERM, why worry about risks that may have no effect on our major goals and objectives. The best way to focus your risk identification efforts is to establish the context and rationale for ERM as we have described in Chapter 4.

The context defines the boundaries within which the risk exists. Anything outside of those boundaries may not be important to consider, or at least, not on an immediate basis. Unless your organization has unlimited resources, you will realize a far greater benefit by focusing on the risks that may impact you the most.

You need to begin by establishing the context:

- Why are we in existence?
- What are the most important elements of our mission and vision?
- What are the most important goals and strategies that will enable achieve those elements?
- What the greatest risk to those goals and strategies?

The process of establishing the context and most important risks should involve as many individuals within the organization as practicable. At a minimum, it should include the Board of Directors, the Executive Director, key operational staff. The process should result in a clear set of risks which are most important to be mitigated so the organization can achieve expected outcomes.

For example, if your mission is to serve the young people in jeopardy of being involved with drugs, one of your more important goals may be providing an effective counseling service to those people. If you have limited staff, one of your more important strategies then, may be to make effective use of volunteers. Then one of your most significant risks may be lack of volunteers who are sufficiently trained in dealing with addiction. If this risk comes to fruition, your goal of providing effective counseling could be at risk.

Those who are being asked to identify risks should be given some guidance on how to identify relevant risks.

There are two primary approaches for looking for risks: a functional approach which looks at the operational aspects of the organization (such as the ones describe in the previous example), and a dynamic approach, which deals with environmental factors such as socio-economic, political and climatic conditions. Each enables a comprehensive means of identifying risk by looking at risk from major these vantage points. Using both methods enhances the overall identification process.

Functional Approach

The functional approach looks at risk that can be associated directly with the operational functions such as accounting or volunteer management. In large nonprofits, there may be a group of individuals dedicated to certain functions like these. In smaller organizations, however, one individual may have the responsibility of handling multiple operational responsibilities. In these smaller organizations, it is important that different functions, like bookkeeping and volunteer management, be looked at separately.

There are a few different ways to look at functional operations with respect to risk:

- Strategic or tactical plans that are dependent on a specific function
  - › Example: The strategy may call for a significant increase in the fund development – what risks exist for this to be actualized.
- Strategic or tactical plans that may present a risk to one or more functions

> Example: If the strategy calls for doubling the number of volunteers and the person responsible for volunteer management also does the bookkeeping – what is the risk that the staff person will be able to handle both?

- Risks inherent to the function

  > Example: Technology obsolescence or loss of human intellectual property through the attrition – what is the risk of this impacting the function and the organization overall?

- Risks external to the organization that may have an impact on the function

  > Example: An incident occurs that diminishes the reputation of the organization – what is the risk that this could have a significant downward effect on fund development.

Dynamic Approach

The dynamic approach looks at the environment within which the organization exists. Again, establishing the context for risk is critically important, as it will help you consider the dynamics of the environment within which the organization exists.

Here are a few categories of dynamics facing most organization:

- Past issues/risks faced by the functional area

  > Example: A change in the economy or the political environment that had an impact on fund development.

- Impending socioeconomic changes and trends

  > Example: A change in attitudes about supporting a certain cause that could result in a reduction of contributions.

- Potential trends from one egregious occurrence
  › Example: A volunteer is crippled or seriously injured while providing service as a result of poor maintenance of equipment or facilities that results in a reduction of volunteers.
- Benchmark data
  › Example: Major shifts in population over time that could significantly increase the number of individuals the organization is committed to serve and creates a resource availability risk.

Once the type of risks your organization may face is determined, you may find it helpful to group individually identified risks together into categories. Categorizing risk will help to both provide a common understanding of the nature of all the risks as well as help when developing mitigation processes, as a number of smaller individual risks might be mitigated one major mitigation action plan.

Establishing categories will also better ensure completeness during the identification process. As your organization begins to determine the risks within the categories it will become more apparent when a risk(s) is overlooked. Risk categories may differ from organization to organization. The following is sample list of risk categories you may be helpful:

Twelve sample categories:

Information Technology	Agency Operations
Agency Staff (HR)	Volunteers (HR)
Marketing and Outreach	Volunteer Management
Donor Relationships	Reputation
Fund Development	Legal
Governance	Overall Strategic Plan Risk

For example, using the example we provided above, if your mission is to serve the young people at risk of being involved with drugs and one of your more important goals is providing effective counseling services, you might ask a question related to each of these categories:

- Information Technology Risk

  › Do we have an up-to-date database of at-risk youth?

- Agency Staff Risk

  › Do we have a sufficient number of staff to handle the community we are committed to serve?

- Marketing and Outreach Risk:

  › Are we effectively getting out our message?

- Donor Relationship Risk

  › Do we have a strong relationship with the donor community most sympathetic to this issue?

- Fund Development Risk

  › How likely is it that we will be able to raise sufficient funding?

- Governance Risk

  › Are internal agency operations functioning properly?

- Agency Operations Risk

  › Are volunteers trained, background checked, certified, bonded or otherwise qualified to provide services to our clients?

- Reputational Risk

  › What is our reputation?

- Legal Risk

  › Have we considered all the legal ramifications of the services we are providing?

- Strategic Plan Risk

  › Are there any other elements of our strategic plan that could present a risk to this strategy?

Not all categories will be relevant or important to all strategies and objectives. But by having the list, you are more likely not to miss any that are.

A sample of these risk categories with descriptions can be found in Appendix 2.

ERM Process Point 2: Prioritize

Prioritize

As previously mentioned, the number of risks an organization face is literally incalculable. Any attempt to identify and address every conceivable risk would leave an organization with no resources to do to anything else. Clearly, there needs to be a way to prioritize risk so that the most important ones can be identified and dealt with.

Prioritizing risk

As previously mention, start by asking what is your most important goal or strategy? Ask yourself a couple of questions:

- If there was only one thing you wanted to get done this year, what would that be?

- What is the one goal or strategy that ensure your organization will survive, or even thrive?

- Which of the many risks you face could prevent your organization from reaching its strategic goals and objectives?

Your objective should be to determine the all the risks that will affect this goal, and then how significant each of those risks are. Primed with the risks that survive this first pass, next come several other criteria. These include:

- How soon is the risk likely to materialize?

- Will the risk be repetitive?

- What is its intensity?

Answers to these questions should help you determine, how much you do to mitigate the risk and how soon you need to do something.

But how do you measure this?

Scales for the Enterprise

Prioritizing risk involves measuring the likelihood of any particular risk and evaluating the impact or consequence of that risk occurring. By taking such measurements you will develop a set of coordinates (likelihood score, impact score) that can be used to plot a point on the axes of a typical heat map, or other chart to help establish priorities. (See example in the Appendix.)

But even without formally preparing a heat map, the process of scoring each risk should readily reveal which risks areas most important to deal with first. By scoring each risk, it should become clear that ones have a greater likelihood of occurring, and will have a great or lesser impact or consequence than another. Obviously, it is important to document your risks, triage and deal with the most significant sooner rather than later.

So, where do you begin?

Measuring likelihood and impact involves the use of scales, which can be as simple as using terms such as "high," "medium," and "low"; or more sophisticated as in using numerical scales, such as "1-3," "1-5" or "1-100." Experience shows that the simpler the scale, the easier it will be for the individuals involved in measuring likelihood and impact to arrive at a score. We recommend using the 1-5 scale, which provides a combination of simplicity and some granularity and choice.

There is one problem with a five point scale. Too many people try to use the middle number 3 to avoid what could be interpreted as the extremes. If that occurs, a simple solution is to force rank all the risks and a leader or moderator picks where to draw the line for those risks that will be a 1, 2, 3, 4 or 5. OK, that's the easy part.

The difficulty arises in determining the score. There are two primary methods: quantitative scoring and qualitative scoring.

Quantitative scoring is relatively simple. For example, the risk is likely to happen next week or a year from now and will result in some measurable impact, such as dollars lost or increased costs.

Unfortunately not all risks are measurable in such terms. The lion's share of risks need to be measured in more qualitative terms. It is difficult, if not impossible, to measure issues such as reputational risk or donor attitudes in hard dollars or other numerical terms.

Issues such as these boil down to good old-fashioned business judgment. "Employee morale is at an all-time low" or "social tensions are more intense than they have ever been" are common qualitative ways of scoring risk. Certainly, organizations can use methods such as board surveys or complex actuarial models to try and establish a numeric score. For example, a survey could reveal that nine out of 10 staff members are upset with the salary freeze that will be imposed. But such tools often require a significant amount of time and money; and in many cases, they simply substantiate common sense or intuitive judgment. Business judgment often comes into play when determining the likelihood and impact of risk. The question then becomes how to turn such judgments or estimations into something quantifiable. Judgment, after all, is in the eye of the beholder. A risk that one person sees as "the sky is falling" may be viewed by another as merely negligible. But this variability can be overcome.

Enter the Jellybean – Leveling the Playing Field Across the Enterprise

In 2007, Michael Mauboussin presented a big jar of jellybeans to his 73 Columbia Business School students.[1] How many beans did they think it contained?

Student estimates ranged from 250 to 4,100; the actual number was 1,116. Those estimates produced a collective error rate of 700—a massive 62%—demonstrating that individually the students were poor estimators. What is interesting, however, is that the average guess was 1,151, just 3% off the mark. Even more startling, only two of the 73 students' guesses were better than the group average.

So, while each individual student was way off in his or her estimate, collectively the group was very accurate. The message here is take everyone's point of view and average it out to a reasonable degree. The average will be closer to reality than any individual potentially biased opinions will be.

Michael Mauboussin concluded that:

"… a diverse crowd will always predict more accurately than the average individual. So the crowd predicts better than the people in it. Not sometimes - Always. [And] collective predictive ability is equal parts accuracy and diversity." [2].

The analog can be applied to establishing a score for judging the likelihood and impact of each risk. By assembling a representative group of individuals from the organization—it could be the executive director and senior staff—that group can collectively determine how to scale each major risk. But here's where the opportunity to involve others may come into play. Subordinate staff, who are involved in the day to day details, or Board members, who you would expect to have a very broad purview, may be able to provide a lot insight too. It is wise to get them involved, make them part of the process, get their buy-in.

At this point let's hit the "pause button" and ask an important question: Is the risk that is being assessed one that directly relates to a key element of the organization's strategy? Or has the process devolved into trying to measure every known risk the organization faces? If it is the former, you are assessing a risk that is straight to the point, i.e. a risk that is truly significant right now. If it is the latter, then you are getting too bogged down to reach a meaningful result.

Do not let your quantification slow the process too much. Remember the jellybean story.

Determine the Scales to be used

Each organization should set its own scales. There will be no national standards of benchmarks that will be more meaningful than one you establish for yourself. For example, if a large organization loses 25 donors, the impact may not be a big deal, (unless they are large donors). If a small organization loses 25, it could mean the difference between survival and failure. So, for a large organization the loss of 25 donors may get rated as a "1" on a scale from 1-5 with 5 being the greatest impact. For the smaller a loss of 25 might get rated as a "5" on the same scale.

Once these scales are established, they should be used consistently across the organization to measure the risk. For example, the risk to this particular goal or objective is "X". if we don't mitigate risk "X", it is highly likely (on a scale of 1-5 where 5 is high) to result in a significant loss of donors, (where significant is specifically relevant to this organization).

Once the scale ranges are determined they should be used to assess and prioritize risks. It will be necessary to develop a definition of the scale and to use that definition consistently across the organization.

While these scales need to be used consistently across the organization It is often difficult to use the same measurement for all situations. For example, the likelihood of a specific event occurring, like a change to tax laws or the retirement of key staff may be able to be measured in terms of a period of time such as month or years but a period of time doesn't work so well for risks such as donor relations or reputational risk. Risks such as these might be better measured in terms of intensity. For example, the likelihood of our reputation affecting this risk is at an all-time low (meaning you enjoy and excellent reputation at this point in time). Thus, you may need slightly different measurement criteria depending on the category of risk. The following three are recommended:

Likelihood scoring: Timeframe, Frequency, Intensity

• **Timeframe**—used for risk factors that can be measured in terms of time. For example, is the risk likely to occur next week, or sometime within the next five years? The score applied to a more immediate risk would be high; those further in the future would be low.

• **Frequency**—used to determine the level of risk based on how often that risk may occur. An event that occurs often would be scored as a high; those that occur more seldom would be scored as a low.

• **Intensity**—used for risk factors that cannot, or are best not, measured in terms of when or how often they will occur. For example, reputational risk is ever present. And when they occur, their effect can last a very long time. They can only be determined by level or intensity. (See Appendix 3 for sample likelihood scales.)

Impact scoring: Level of Severity

Determining the likelihood of a risk is not enough. The bottom-line impact, or a proxy for it, is also needed.

Impact can be described in terms such as loss of funding, increased costs, number of volunteers, or number of individuals that can be served. Different operational functions may look at the impact in different quantitative ways. For example, the fund development function may evaluate the impact of donor loss in terms of dollars or percentage of revenue, while the public relations function may view this same loss in terms of the organization's image or reputation. (See Appendix 3 for sample impact scales.)

Whatever scales are used, and however the likelihood and impact are measured, the result should provide you with a prioritized list of the risks, which will enable you to determine what you work on first in your mitigation plan.

ERM Process Point 3: Mitigate

Mitigate

Developing Business-Process Based Risk Mitigation

A common approach to risk mitigation is to develop and implement a control. While few would deny the importance of controls, in reality, most nonprofits have both limited staff and time available to design and implement a complex set of controls that could wind up bogging them down in the delivery of the services they are providing to their community.

There are certainly some operations that lend themselves easily to controls. Financial operations, for example. Having a segregation of duties whenever possible over the receipt and recording of donations and the disbursement of those funds, is clearly something that can and should be implemented.

But how about other risk, like reputational risks or technology obsolescence? In both of these examples, controls are difficult to employ.

You often hear people say "my computer is getting slow". Unlike some of us, a computer's processing power never actually slows down with age. But it may be that the amount of data that's being processed due to an expanding constituent base has increased over time and this takes older processors longer to handle. Or, more and more of your organization's processes are now online, making the technology you have appear to be slow. You can't control your technology infrastructure from aging but you may periodically reassess whether or not it is adequate for your needs.

If you provide some level of personal service to your constituents, like counseling or life guidance, it may be impossible to control the actions of staff or volunteers who are providing these services on a day-to-day basis. If one or more of your staff misguides a client, it could result in a reputational risk. So, although a control may not be practical, perhaps a program of regular and required training for staff and volunteers could minimize the potential for a reputational risk.

If ERM is to be integral to an organization's culture, a better approach than simply implementing controls is to determine how the business processes underlying the risk can be enhanced or modified to address that risk. When a risk is identified, the first step is to ask, what are the business processes associated with the risk?

For example, what if a strategic decision is made to expand care for the homeless to provide for overnight shelter. Risk related to this new strategy needs to be considered from two perspectives.

First, what will be the effect of this expanded service on existing processes? Does this service expansion place any additional burden on existing staff, volunteers or facilities? What other services does this new service put at risk, or stated another way, will any other service suffer as a result of the added burden of this new service?

Second, what risks will this new service face that may have an effect on the successful expected outcome of this strategy?

Considering the set of risk categories previously mentioned, risks may be identified from both of these perspectives.

For example:

Technology Risk

- Will this new or expanded service have an impact on the technology needs of existing services?

- Is the technology in place sufficient to handle the potential additional processing requirements of the new or expanded service?

Agency Operations

- Are there a sufficient number of staff or volunteers on hand to handle the additional work load?

- Are there new operational processes that need to be established to address the needs of the expanded service?

Agency Staff and Volunteers

- Will this new service take staff and/or volunteers away from existing roles and responsibilities?

- Will staff need additional training or guidance to be able to deal with this new responsibility.

Each of the risk categories should be considered for this new strategy in terms of what risk it may present to current operations and the organization as a whole, as well as considering the risks the new strategy item may face in terms of its own success.

Precisely how each of the risks in these examples is mitigated will depend entirely on and will be unique to each individual organization. There is no silver bullet or standard means of mitigating any risk. The important point is for the organization to formally address each of these risks well before they occur, as opposed to crossing those bridges when they come to them. The emphasis should be on what processes are in place now and will they be sufficient to deal with the identified risk or how should existing processes be enhanced to address potential risk.

ERM Process Point 4: Report

Monitor and Report: Is the Risk Environment Changing?

One of the most important elements of the ERM process is monitoring the risk environment and communicating the changes in that environment to enable action prior to the occurrence of a risk.

For most organizations, the risk environment is in a constant state of change. Changes may be small or large, come quickly or develop over a long period of time. These changes may create new risks or alter the impact or likelihood of an identified risk. In all cases, however, change inevitably alters risk within an organization.

Monitoring and communications are the keys to any successful ERM program. It is essential to understand how these changes affect the organization, and how to respond to them before the risk occurs. What matters most is having a constant awareness of these changes through effective monitoring.

Each organization needs to establish a champion or central point of contact for risk. This person, and it could be a member of the board, executive director or senior staff should be responsible for periodically checking on the state of risk. Are things changing? Have we made progress on implementing mitigation plans? Are there any signs of impending risk for those risks identified as most likely to occur?

The role of the champion should be to help avoid being surprised by know risks and potential new risks that had not previously been identified. As the risk environment changes, there should be regular communication to the board and ED, and staff as they may be involved. Communication flow should travel in both directions. From the champion to others and from others to the champion. By staying apprised of the risk, the organization will be better able to handle the risk.

ERM Process Point 5: Measure

Measure

Measure: Are we meeting with success?

One way to achieve success is to fully implement the mitigation plans in place for key risks. A robust ERM process entails monthly or quarterly measure of the progress toward fulfilling all the risk mitigation plans in place.

Another way to look at success is to measure the value ERM creates for the enterprise.

Among the benefits of an ERM program are:

- **Creating strategic plans that that are more likely to succeed.** When an organization takes the time to think through all the risks that might impede success of the strategic plan and then follows through with well-defined actions to help reduce or mitigate those risks, the organization should have a higher chance of achieving expected outcomes. Is undertaking a thorough review of potential risks a guarantee the plan will succeed? No. it will still take all the hard work the organization would put into the plan activities even if no risk were considered, but if you know where all the potential pot holes are in the road, you are more steer around them.

- **Understanding the organization's risks holistically.** Not only are both insurable and non-insurable risks identified in ERM, but also their combined potential impact should they occur simultaneously. Further, risks which truly correlated are also identified.

- **Being better able to communicate confidently and quickly about risks facing the organization, regardless of whether the communication is internal or external.** Such communication is a major factor considering the high importance of risk to boards of directors, staff, donors, or other stakeholders in the organization.

- **Being better able to deal with the unknown.** Some risks will always remain unknown and/or interconnections among risks never recognized. However, by working towards mitigating the risks you know, you will be better able to deal with the unknown.

- **Avoiding surprises.** Some surprises are inevitable. Most can be avoided, however, within a risk conscious culture, which emanates from a well-executed ERM process.

Benefits by Stakeholder

The benefits of a well-functioning ERM process go beyond helping the organization achieve its strategic goals and objectives. The following is a summary of who else benefits:

The Board of Directors

- Obtains a macro view of risk across the enterprise

- Understands and can opine on management's view of risk priorities

- Is provided with:

  › A broad view of measures in place to mitigate risk

  › A foundation for a common dialog with management on risk

The Executive Director

- Obtains a composite view of risks

- Is provided a view of mitigation in place

- Is provided with an insight to operational staffs' views of risk

Staff

- Obtain understanding of risks under their responsibility

- Obtain understanding of how risk is managed in other areas of the organization

- Gain insight into risk management best practices across the organization

The Organization

- Develops a well-defined risk culture that can instill great confidence in the organization's continued success

Benefit to the strategic Planning Process

Perhaps one of the greatest benefits of an ERM initiative is when it is used during the planning process. Each year when strategies are developed, or during the course of the year when strategies are updated or changed, risks that have been identified through the ERM process should be considered. Identifying the specific risks that could impede the achievement of strategic goals will ensure that current and new plans are more likely to succeed and goals and objectives of the business plan are achieved.

Value and Taking Credit

Because ERM democratizes risk—each staff member or volunteer is responsible to some extent for managing risk—everyone can take credit for ERM that is successful. When any has performed the steps in the ERM process well, it should to point to qualitative and quantitative benefits that it has brought to bear on the enterprise as a whole. And, it should celebrate its accomplishments and take credit for them.

Taking credit does not mean grandstanding. Rather, it means presenting a status report on ERM which recognizes the contributions of all the parties to any success. On the other hand, status reports sometimes show that performance has not been positive. Thus, those who are involved in managing risk must recognize less than stellar results. When such a situation occurs, the result should be accompanied by what will be done to improve the process or results in the future.

Chapter 8

Typical Risks Faced by Nonprofits

Nonprofits have both insurable and non-insurable risks. In this chapter we will discuss both kinds of risks with the aim providing a long list of risks nonprofits should consider so that they do not focus too heavily on one or two risks while ignoring some others that may be just as dangerous. In the next chapter, we will discuss mitigation tactics for many of these risks.

Strategic Risks

In thinking about strategic risks, it is expedient to think in terms of five fundamental elements that a nonprofit would consider when creating its strategy.

What is the mission i.e. product or service being offered

Who is it for, who benefits, who is the client

How will the mission be funded

Now, what are the kinds of risks that might attach to each of these strategic elements. They will be different for every organization but there are some which tend to be applicable to just about any nonprofit.

Risks Related To Mission/Services/Product

The services that the organization offers can be impacted by change and other factors. Changes may have to do with the client base's needs and wants, legal restrictions or requirements and other external forces. Risk can come out of service execution issues perpetrated by the organization itself. Any of these, if unaddressed, could damage the sustainability of the organization.

Some key risks associated with service include:

- other organizations are entering the area to provide the same or similar services,

- the want or need that the organization was meant to fill is diminishing,

- the cost to provide the service is escalating faster than funds available to cover costs,

- licensing or other legal or regulatory requirements for providing the service are becoming more difficult to meet.

Risks Related To Clients

Demographic, societal, cultural changes that used to happen over many decades can now happen in a matter of a couple of years. For that reason, the profile of the client that the organization's mission was designed to serve can change dramatically in a short space of time. If that happens, there is a risk or uncertainty around whether the organization will continue to be viable or will need to change its strategy.

Some of the key risks that relate to clients:

- the population of people who fit the client profile is currently growing or declining,

- external conditions are changing which may cause the client population to grow or decline in the near future,

- client preferences are changing, they want more privacy in accessing services or they need services provided at different hours, etc.

- transportation to and from where the organization's service is provided is becoming an issue for clients, it is being discontinued or becoming too expensive,

- clients have more choices in terms of where and how to get their needs met, so utilization is decreasing,

- the client base is beginning to find it too hard to pay the small fees involved in utilizing the organization's services.

Risks Related To Funding

Funds are the life blood of the organization. Risks to the funding stream is among the most significant risks an organization can face and it is a strategic risk. Without a plan for who, how and how much revenue must be raised, a nonprofit is on shaky ground. What are the key risks that put funding in jeopardy, they include:

- the economy goes into recession and donors are not as able or willing to donate,

- one large donor's contribution makes up an inordinate percentage of all funding and that donor gets disenchanted and stops giving, decides to spread donations among more organizations and reduces giving, gets "donor fatigue" or dies without leaving the nonprofit in the will,

- federal, state, or local government reduces its funding in part or whole

- other funding source, e.g. United Way, is not raising as much as before and may reduce its funding,

- tax law changes make giving less attractive to would-be donors,

- reputational issues with your organization, or with nonprofits overall, negatively affect giving levels,

- other nonprofits in the area do capital campaigns at the same your organization starts its campaign or announces its major annual fundraiser,

- the national organization, if there is one, increases its association fees putting pressure on local fundraising,
- board is unable or unwilling to do any fund raising.

Other Risks

Any risk that could seriously threaten the ability of the organization to achieve its strategy and meet its objectives is important. That is why the ERM process always starts with an understanding of the strategy. However, not every risk emanates out of the strategy as the ones above do. Some emanate from operations, human resources, the macro-environment, and other areas.

Risks Related To Operations

Nonprofits tend not to have many of the resources that for-profits or large corporations do. As such, they do not often have the monitoring processes and controls in place to ensure the quality, efficiency, or effectiveness of what they do or the service they deliver. Among the risks they face in this regard are:

- technology fails causing downtime, lost data, or other issues
- a cyberattack occurs, e.g. data breach, ransomware, etc.,
- new technology or new process had unintended consequence
- staff or volunteers are not properly trained on the organization's technology and processes
- financial goals/standards not being met, e.g. budgets exceeded, surplus capital not created, receivables written off, etc.

- projects, events, or other planned actions are delayed due to operational issues such as poor planning, poor execution, or unexpected events outside the control of the organization

- random accidents occur which affect staff, volunteers or clients

- something happens which negatively affects the quality of service, the reputation of the organization or cause some other type of damage

- opportunities are lost due to lack of focus or slow response time

Knowing what the risks are, allows organizations to put preventive or mitigation actions in place. In thinking through what the most likely risks are for a given organization, the next step of addressing it becomes natural and logical but not always easy. However, with even limited resources, there needs to be accountability for ensuring that the operations of the organization are running as they should be.

Risks Related To Human Resources

- volunteers do not perform effectively putting the reputation of the nonprofit in jeopardy or exposing the organization to fines, lawsuits, etc.

- staff does not perform effectively putting the reputation of the nonprofit in jeopardy or exposing the organization to fines, lawsuits, etc.

- succession planning for key roles, e.g. Executive Director, Development Director, CFO is haphazard

- staff or volunteers deliberately commit fraud

- staff or volunteers do something illegal

- staff or volunteers ignore safety rules, have accidents

- staff or volunteers sue the organization,

- excessive turnover disrupts organization's operations

- non-compliance with federal, state or local labor and/or employment laws leads to fines, backpay, lawsuits

- lack of adequate training (see above)

Risks Related To The General Environment

The overall socio-economic and climatic environment can have a direct impact on the degree of risk nonprofits face. If litigiousness is rising nationally or locally, it will increase the chance for nonprofits to face lawsuits too, if climate change is affecting properties and operations, it will affect nonprofits as well.

Risks from the external world can pose risks such as:

- reduction in the size of the volunteer pool,

- greater likelihood of suits concerning human resource actions, service issues, workplace injuries,

- workplace violence,

- property damage due to storms or other environmental factors,

- interruption of service due to any external condition,

- cyber breaches, identity theft, cyber ransom, denial of service attacks

- inflation,

- additional local, state or federal regulation,

- tax changes that affect giving.

Conclusion

The lists above are not comprehensive. They serve as a limited illustration of the diversity and significance of risks nonprofits do face and should manage. The primary options for managing risk are:

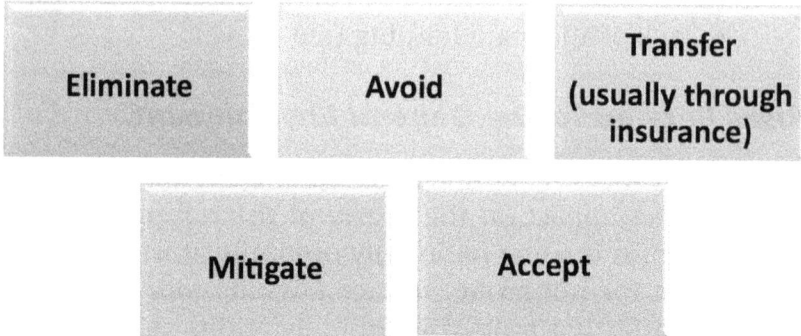

Eliminate

Avoid

Transfer (usually through insurance)

Mitigate

Accept

In the next chapter we will discuss mitigation techniques. Keep in mind that even acceptance of risk should not mean ignoring it completely. If an organization accepts an important risk exist and decides it can or will do nothing to prevent it, it still needs to monitor the progression of the risk in the event it morphs or grows into something that cannot be accepted. The risk may dissolve on its own or may persist and materialize into the death knell for the organization.

Chapter 9

Mitigation Tactics

Mitigation is the singular most important step in the process of managing risk. It is one thing to identify and understand risk, but if no steps are taken to reduce the risk, all the effort put into the process thus far are for naught.

It may also be the most difficult step in your overall efforts to manage risk. For the most part, each risk will be unique to each organization, so there is no standard solution that applies to every nonprofit that can be drawn on and implemented. Within an organization, how one risk is managed will likely be different than how another risk is managed.

To effectively mitigate an organization's risk, any individual steps taken to mitigate risk should be part of an overall plan. There may be instances where the mitigation process for one risk also provides some help with another, but it is also possible that taking steps to reduce risk in one area has the unintended consequence of increasing the risk in another. Suffice it to say, that risk mitigation must be looked at comprehensively across the organization as a whole.

A mitigation plan must, of course be based on the results of the identification and analysis of risk. During those phases, risks were identified and prioritized based on the likelihood and potential impact or consequence to the organization. The mitigation plan should follow those priorities and deal with the most significant risks first.

There are a number of ways to mitigate risk. For example, a simple control such as segregation of duties might be a good way to mitigate financial risk. You can transfer risk through obtaining Insurance coverage to reduce your liabilities. You can also decide that the risk is either too small to worry about, or so unsolvable there is absolutely nothing you can do to reduce the risk. But even in these last two scenarios, being aware of the possibility of something occurring is better than being caught by complete surprise. So, in a way, even if you do nothing, you have mitigated the risk to some degree if for nothing else, you are prepared to brace yourself.

The good news is that adding a control, transferring the risk or taking no action are simple steps to take. The bad news is that for the most part, they only help in a limited number of situations and typically in the area pf financial risk. Risks such as the loss of a key individual or the risk of the loss of a major funding source do not lend themselves to simple controls, nor is it easy to transfer those risk to through insurance.

These types of risks need to be addressed through the development of or enhancement of organizational process. In fact, the majority of your risk will likely need to be mitigated by a business process.

When a risk is identified, the first step is to ask, what are the business processes associated with the risk?

For example, what is the existing process for obtaining a grant? How many people are involved? Are the requests reviewed by more than one person? Are the requests logged and tracked for future follow-up?

For each of these elements, there is an implied control. If multiple people are involved in the development of grant requests, the risk of poorly constructed requests may be reduced, if requests are reviewed by a final uninvolved set of eyes. This may reduce the risk of errors and omissions within the request or simply improve the overall quality of the request, thus reducing the risk of the grant not being obtained. If the requests are properly documented in a log, the risk of not following up on them on a timely basis or the risk of simply missing key dates will be reduced.

The very first step in mitigation necessarily involves reviewing and documenting the processes involved within the area where the risk exists. Are there any weak points in the process? Can the process be streamlined or made more efficient, thereby reducing the risk of simply running out of time to complete the work? It may seem a tedious effort to document each step of an operation yet by simply writing the steps down, any shortcomings in the process should become immediately apparent. In addition, having processes documented can be quite helpful when a new person comes into the organization, or if someone needs to fill in during a planned or unforeseen absence or to ensure that more than one individual within the organization is aware of how an operational process is done, should the person with the primary responsibility for that process unexpectedly leave.

During the process of documenting the operation, the following questions should be asked:

1. Who is involved in the process?

2. Does any part of or all of the process involve a computer or IT system?

3. Does this process depend on other processes within the organization?

4. Is the process dependent upon individuals external to the organization?

5. Are other organizational process depend on this process?

6. Who is accountable for the proper operation of the process?

7. Can the process be simplified?

By asking yourself these question during a review of the process, you should be able to identify specific points in the process that relate directly to the risks that surfaced during the identification and analysis phases. Once these risks are understood, you will more easily find ways to mitigate the risk through a control, transference, a change to the process or you may simply come to the conclusion that nothing can be done. It is from this analysis that you will build the elements of your overall mitigation plan.

Although it will be impossible to discuss mitigation steps for all for the potential areas of risk within a nonprofit, and although no two nonprofits will ever be identical with respect to risk, there are two areas that will most likely be common to all: fund development and loss of key personnel.

Let's take a look at both areas individually and see what type of risk may exist and what mitigation processes may be employed.

Fund Development Risk Mitigation

Activities involved in fund development can range from solicitations from individual or organizational donors to complex application for grants from government sources or large foundations whose mission is to distribute funds they have raised such as the Bill & Melinda Gates Foundation.

In general fund development may contain a number of risks not only within the development process itself, but to other aspects of the organization.

The following is a list of possible risks and suggestions for mitigation.

Fund Development Operational Risk

- Funds are solicited from unreliable sources.

  › Rank sources based on likelihood of funds being received to set expectations for financial planning. e.g. "we only expect 50% of the targeted funds to be received from source X."

  › Score each source of funding by likelihood of funds being received, on a scale of 1 – 5 for example. This will help you determine which sources are at greatest risk of loss and allow you to focus efforts on successfully obtaining those funds

- Grants requests are incomplete or not followed up on a timely basis.

  › All grant requests over X dollars are reviewed by a second person or the Executive Director

- Restricted funds are not appropriately identified.

  › Fund accounting system enhancements

- Loss of one or more major donors

  › Determine downstream operational impact of loss and identify or rank programs to be adjusted or suspended

- Grants are not renewed as expected

  › Determine the likelihood of grant rejections and plan accordingly, also always ask for details about why grant was denied to mitigate future denials

- IT systems that support fund development fail or are cannot support operational requirements

  › Require planned upgrades to systems or equipment that support fund development

- Data is lost

  › Establish data backup and restore procedures

- A data breach occurs resulting in unauthorized disclosure of funding sources or a violation of donor privacy

  › Periodic review of security over physical and automated fund record keeping

- IT systems crash or are physically destroyed by disaster

  › Business continuity plan for all automated fund management processes

Fund Development Financial Risk

- Estimates built into organizational plans are impacted by unexpected external or internal conditions such as economic downturn or Inflation increases expenses more than anticipated in budgets

  › Crisis rank agency services and associated personnel to quickly determine reductions in services or staff that will have the least impact on mission goals and objectives

  › Review related expenses and prioritize expenditure to be able to quickly alter plans

- Accounting, processing errors or Insufficient audit oversight

> › Follow generally accepted accounting procedures for management of funds, including periodic internal audits

Fund Development Regulatory Risk

- Escalation of scrutiny of grant requests due to increase competition for funds

  › Monitor growth in the number of potential competitors for funding source and differentiate your requests

  › Monitor State and Federal developments related to Nonprofits for potential changes and lobby as effectively as practical

Fund Development Reputational Risk

- An action by a volunteer causes harm to reputation of agency causing a reduction of funds

  › Establish policies and standards for services to be performed and ensure providers are appropriately trained and refreshed

  › Develop standards and have contractual agreements for moral and ethical behavior by staff and volunteers and with periodic renewal

- Services provided fall short of donor expectations

  › Periodic survey of donor expectations and whether or not they are being met

  › Periodic retraining of volunteers and staff who perform services

- Community attitudes change with respect to the mission of the agency

  › Monitor social attitudes and how agency services measure up

- Naming rights given for some aspect of the nonprofit to someone who becomes a "persona non grata" to the general public

  › Aim for naming rights that are not from those who are not overly prominent in the public eye in case they misdeed.

Fund Development Geopolitical Risk

- Changes in political party in control of sources of government grants or Reductions in Federal, State or local allocations for nonprofit expenditures

  › Ensure advocacy programs are in place to help new legislative bodies understand importance of funding

  › Ultimately, there may be little that any one agency can do to alter the course of policy in this regard. The one thing that can be done is careful monitoring of the geopolitical environment so that the agency is not caught by surprise and can make appropriate adjustments to services or other sources of funding to adjust for potential loss of funds.

Loss of Key Personnel

One of the other areas that can have a significant impact on an organization is the loss of key staff members or of the executive director her or himself. The loss of these individuals may be planned or expected such as in the case of retirement or it can occur as the result of an unexpected and often unfortunate circumstance such as the individuals untimely passing.

Whether anticipated or unexpected, sound succession planning can help an organization more effectively deal with the resulting transition.

Little can be more disruptive of accomplishing goals and objective than losing key personnel. First, let's put key personnel into perspective.

Let's face it, unless you are a mega nonprofit with hundreds of staff and volunteers, EVERYONE is key to your success. Whether it be the Executive Director or the newest staff member that you just spent a month training in their new role, the loss of any individual comes with a cost. Mitigating this risk is a matter of minimizing the time or money that will be spent in replacing that individual. And yes, even mega organizations should have a plan to deal with and minimize the consequence of personnel loss.

The likelihood of the loss of personnel can range from individuals leaving for a new job or other personal reasons, planned retirement, to sudden loss due to some tragic event, or even terminations. Mitigation for those losses that come as a surprise are generally outside of the control of any organization, large or small. Retirements or terminations are usually not a surprise and may even be planned. Most of these personal issues are generally dealt with by sound Human Resource management. Sound HR management practices are the first order of mitigation.

Nevertheless, key person losses will happen and you can mitigate or reduce the degree to which the event impacts your organization.

The loss of any individual will cause the processes of an organization to slow down. The major objective of risk mitigation should be to prevent the organization grinding to a halt as well as to get the organization back up and running normally, as quickly as possible. The simplest way to reduce the impact is by having a succession plan.

Succession plans generally have two aspects. One is the development of new leaders who can replace key personnel when they leave, retire or die. The other is to ensure that someone is prepared to assume the roles of others within the organization as the need arises. All organizations need both.

While the degree of plan detail may vary significantly from the ED to the staff person, the plans should address both the development of individuals to potentially fill those roles and clear and readily available documentation of the duties performed.

The first part, personnel development, should be managed by the individual or group of individuals responsible for Human Resources. We will not attempt to cover all the elements of sound HR practices here other than to say the organization should have some. If you don't, you will be leaving yourself vulnerable not only to the risk of not being able to replace or promote from within but also to the risk of operational tasks not being performed as well as they should be.

Another aspect is more operational in nature. Just exactly what does each person do? How much of what she or he does is in the person's head as opposed to being documented? Especially in small organizations, and especially when the person has been in their role for an extended period of time, the person sees no reason to write the process down. In addition, even if procedures were once documented, those processes are likely to have changed, perhaps significantly, over long periods of time.

Despite it being a considerable task, every job process needs to be written down. What needs to be documented are actually two things. The first is a simple job description, what duties or responsibilities does the role perform. The second, and possibly more important, is how is the job done – what are the process steps.

The first part is useful in setting performance evaluation criteria, pay scales and other normal Human Resource functions. The second is the "how to" instructions that someone who needs to quickly assume those responsibilities will need to have in order to do the work.

So, what are some of the basic elements of a good succession plan?

- Clear job descriptions so you know the skills, abilities, and experience needed to perform the function.

- A list of other individuals who could perform that role if necessary.

- A method to communicate changes to processes and procedures within that job function.

- Effective employee onboarding process and ongoing training.

- Use of coaching, mentoring, and feedback.

- Exit interviews to understand why people leave and any changes that might have occurred in performing the work.

- A schedule to periodically update operational procedures.

Job Descriptions	Training	Organization
Documented Procedures & Processes	Workshops	Charts
Automated systems & AI	Employee Meetings	Succession Plans
	Performance Reviews	Efficient Hiring Process

Chapter 10

Tips On Creating Your Insurance Program

Even the smallest of nonprofits will likely need some insurance. Going without, would be a very risky proposition, indeed. There is no single insurance template for organizations to use because every organization will have its own unique set of insurance needs. In fact, most nonprofits will seek the advice of an agent or broker to help them sort out exactly what coverage is needed.

Choosing the Agent or Broker

The first thing to consider is who will choose the agent or broker to consult. Typically, such decisions are the remit of Board, the Chief Financial Officer, or Chief Risk Officer, if there is one.

The next thing is to create a list of criteria to use in selecting the right the agent or broker. Here is a list of criteria to illustrate the point.

- Integrity – What is their reputation, what do they say about their values, can they provide references.

- Stability – How long have they been in business, what is their financial situation, are they growing or shrinking, do they have a lot of staff turnover.

- Expertise – does their staff know about and handle all the kinds of insurance needed, e.g. property, casualty, workers compensation, cyber, employee benefits, directors & officers, error & omissions, employment practices liability and others which may be needed, e.g. medical malpractice, aviation, etc.

- Experience – do they have other nonprofit clients, what is their knowledge level about nonprofits.

- Technology – are they up to date with technology, will it be easy to do business with them, will they communicate with you the way you want.

- Auxiliary Services – do they: 1) consult on the type of policy and limits you should consider, 2) do contract reviews, 3) provide side by side comparisons of underwriter submissions, 4) offer any other risk mitigation services.

- Billing – are they commission, or fee based, do they charge extra for auxiliary services, do they provide premium billing options.

Choosing the Carrier

Most agents or brokers will submit applications to several carriers, so they can get at least three quotes to present to the nonprofit for comparison purposes. Of-course price is very important, but it should not be sole determinant. The comparison must first make sure whether the quotes are apples to apples or apples to prunes. Where there are significant differences in 1) limits, 2) exclusions, 3) deductibles, 4) reinstatement premiums and so on, these need to be accounted for in comparing pricing.

Second, the comparison must also consider the insurer's:

- financial strength, e.g. A.M. Best rating, S&P rating, Demotech rating
- claims paying/service reputation
- underwriting and claims turnover
- locations
- auxiliary services and capabilities
- technology
- information transparency

The agent or broker will usually assist significantly in the comparison, but the client nonprofit should be just as involved and be focused on the meaningful details.

Determining Coverage

Organizations must determine what coverage to purchase and that entails decisions about:

- What is required vs what is good to have vs what is nice to have
- Type of policy or coverage
- Deductibles or self-insured retentions
- Limits or amount of coverage
- Endorsements, e.g. additional insured status for another entity
- Exclusions, what are they and are they acceptable

Typical Coverage

- Property – This includes coverage on the property the nonprofit owns, also furniture, equipment, supplies. It can also include data, so if data is lost, corrupted, or made unavailable, the property policy may apply. Every policy is a bit different and the policy language must be reviewed to understand the scope of the coverage. A property policy is not a cyber policy.

- General Liability - This includes coverage if the nonprofit is sued for personal injury, negligence, libel, slander, misrepresentation in advertising as well as other types of suits. It also covers damage to rented property as well as accidents.

- Professional Liability/E&O – If the organization offers a service or product which is professional in nature, e.g. counseling, daycare, mentoring, etc. it will need this type of policy. This would cover losses due to mistakes made or negative inaction on the part of the organization's employees in the performance of their work and finished products.

- Medical Malpractice – This would cover professional services related to healthcare.

- Abuse and Molestation – This would specifically cover in the event of employees abusing or molesting clients of the organization and would likely not be covered in any other policy the organization may have such as the general liability policy.

- Auto – If the nonprofit owns and operates vehicles it will need to have coverage for bodily injury and physical damage events that could occur with the vehicles. The coverage will be written as a commercial auto policy if the vehicle is owned, leased, or borrowed by an organization.

- Workers Compensation – If the nonprofit has employees, it will need workers compensation insurance which covers workers injuries which occur on the job.

- Cyber – This would cover certain expenses in the event of a cyber incident such as hacking/theft of data, ransomware attack, denial of service attack, etc. Cyber policies tend to be unique so, once again, it is important to review the policy wording to ascertain the exact coverage.

- Employment Practices Liability – This would cover defense costs and other losses due to employment related suits such as those related to Title VII discrimination, sexual harassment, FLMA violations, among others. If the organization has no employees, this cover may not be needed.

- Crime – This would cover losses the organization sustains due to theft, fraud or other crimes committed by its employees.

- Fiduciary Liability – This covers claims against the organization due to its management of pay and benefits for its employees.

- Nonprofit Directors and Officers – This would cover the organization and its directors and officers in the event of a suit or damage caused by their routine direction and management of the organization.

- Umbrella – This adds another layer of limits above those in another policy(ies).

Details, Details, Details

The old saying, "the devil is in the details" could not apply more when it comes to the organization's insurance policies. Some hypothetical and real-life examples will provide the case for careful and deliberate design and understanding of the specifics within any insurance contract.

- A small nonprofit holds a fundraiser event at which it offers liquor drinks for sale. One board member asks if the organization is covered should someone drink too much at the event and cause an accident. The Executive Director reminds the board member that they have a general liability policy. This policy may not cover in this circumstance because the drinks were sold not free. The organization may be liable for an accident caused by someone who became intoxicated at its fundraiser because, in many states, a separate liquor liability policy is required.

- A mid-size nonprofit moves its insurance program from one broker to another and with that it changes insurers as well. The new D&O policy is a "claims made" policy just like the last one. The nonprofit is sued by a former employee for wrongful termination during the new policy period and expects the new carrier to cover defense costs. But the new policy had a provision that only applies if the event that gave rise to the claim (i.e. the termination) happened in the new policy period. Therefore, no coverage is afforded, and the organization pays $80,000 in legal bills to defend itself. There are ways to avoid this gap in coverage but the gap would need to be understood first in order to be addressed.

- A mid-size nonprofit collects disability insurance premiums from its employees but it does not pay the insurer for the coverage. It is not clear if the cause of the lack of payment is clerical error or a deliberate act. Two employees become disabled and the disability insurer denies payment. They sue the nonprofit. The organization turns to its insurance policies for coverage but there is none. Without a fiduciary liability policy, it will have to pay any and all costs associated with rectifying the issue.

- A large nonprofit organizes a fundraiser which includes prizes for the professional golfers who participate in the event as well as for fans at the 18th hole who would get $100 each for the first hole-in-one and $500 for the second hole-in-one. Two professionals aced the 137-yard hole and the charity had to pay out almost $200,000 to fans who were at the green. The charity had bought special event coverage for just this sort of situation, but the insurer refused to pay because the policy clearly stated that it only covered holes at least 170 yards long. A federal appeals court ruled in favor of the insurer when the charity sued it for breach of contract. In this example, there was a need for the nonprofit to match the details of its event with the details in the policy it procured. [1]

The best way to make sure you have the insurance you need is to use a broker or agent with nonprofit experience and to ask as many scenario-based questions as you can. For example, would this policy protect us if X happened or Y happened. Only you know the most likely scenarios which may befall your organization even though you cannot predict all of them. Working with your broker, agent, and underwriter, you should be able to craft a comprehensive program that will fit your budget. If cost becomes prohibitive for the program you want, then that is when your ERM process will need to compensate. Are there risks which you must avoid such as not providing a particular service or are there mitigation steps you need to take in lieu of insurance where insurance might have been preferred, and so on.

.

Chapter 11

The Value of ERM

Nonprofits will find that the benefits of applying the ERM process to their organization far outweigh the time and effort. In very small nonprofits, the board may have to own and implement the process whereas in larger nonprofits, it may be the executive director with some staff. In very large nonprofits, there may be a Chief Risk Officer, just as there are in very large for-profit corporations. Whatever the case, knowing and managing risk has value.

The value of a process is measured by the resulting financial or other type of gain the organization derives from the process. Business Process Re-engineering (BPR), for example, focuses on improving the quality of operating processes so that operations are faster, less expensive, and higher quality. ERM focuses on minimizing the negative effects of risks or uncertainties and optimizing the opportunities risks may present.

For some organizations, just the act of implementing ERM is enough. In other words, the value is "understood". For others, it is important to know exactly how much value has been created in quantifiable terms. Below we will look at "understood" value and quantified value.

Measuring Value Illustrations

Intuitive

Consider an organization that identifies the lack of succession planning for the Executive Director and Chief Financial Officer or Treasurer as a risk, then develops a succession plan and updates the plan, as needed. There is no guarantee that at the time of needing to fill one of these key positions everything will go as planned. However, the Board of the organization can reasonably expect the risk has been greatly reduced because it had been identified and addressed. There would be an intuitive recognition of the value of ERM as it relates to peace of mind and a smoother transition in the face of top level turnover.

Quantitative

Next, consider an organization that had identified the lack of a large and diversified enough donor base as a risk. It was doing well enough financially but several large donors made up 50% of its income. It determined the financial impact of the risk of losing two of such donors was equivalent to 15% of its annual budget. After implementing a successful plan of increasing its donor base, the impact of losing two of the original large donors was equivalent to only 4% of their annual budget or the amount of discretional spend. The difference between 15% and 4% of the annual budget could be considered the value of ERM.

More on Quantification

When doing the prioritization of risks, we talked about defining the risk impact. Using risk impact estimates is another means to determine the value of risk management.

Several measures have been discussed for prioritizing risks, impact can serve as the basis for deriving value of avoiding, mitigating, or transferring the risk.

Likelihood: Timeframe, Frequency, Intensity

- Timeframe—used for risk factors that can be measured in terms of time. For example, is the risk likely to occur next week, or sometime within the next five years? The score applied to a more immediate risk would be high; those further in the future would be low.

- Frequency—used to determine the level of risk based on how often that risk may occur. An event that occurs often would be scored as a high; those that occur more seldom would be scored as a low.

- Intensity—used for risk factors that cannot, or are best not, measured in terms of when or how often they will occur. For example, competitive risk, reputational risk, or product-demand risk factors are ever present. And when they occur, they are a constant, not a one- time' or two-time event. They can only be determined by level or intensity.

Impact: Level of Severity

Impact can be described in terms of lost revenue/donations, increased cost, amounts of fines and penalties, reduced corpus, or dips in investment income. There are different ways of looking at impact from the same derivative, for example, fewer people served can mean a loss of fees but can also be looked at as a raw number – fewer people served relative to the organization's mission.

The following equation can be used for any risk whose impact has been estimated:

Risk 1 Value Equation

IMPACT ESTIMATE – COST OF MITIGATION = VALUE OF ERM FOR RISK 1

Practically, this valuing process should be applied to some sub-set of all risks, i.e. the most significant and serious risks faced by the organization.

Common Quantitative Benefits of ERM

These are some of the common and very quantifiable benefits of ERM:

- Reduction in the number of legal suits
- Reduction in the number of workplace accidents
- Reduction in the number of lost work days due to workplace accidents
- Reduction in the number of insurance claims
- Reduction in the cost of insurance claims
- Reduction in the cost of insurance premiums
- Reduction in the total cost of risk (TCOR)
- Reduction in the number of negative financial surprises
- Reduction in the number of negative non-financial surprises
- Avoidance or reduction of fines and penalties of non-compliance with laws, regulations, or contractual obligations
- Improved response time and reduced downtime due to crises, catastrophes

Common Qualitative Benefits of ERM

It should be remembered that the following common qualitative benefits of ERM all have value even if the value is not quantified in numerical terms:

- Greater peace of mind by all stakeholders in the organization

- Improved public image for organization

- Improved employee morale

- Fewer surprises

- Better preparedness in the event of a loss event

- Greater ease in obtaining insurance coverage

- Improved terms for insurance purchased

- Enhanced understanding of the strategy, objectives, and operations of the organization by all those involved in the ERM process

Chapter 12

Nonprofit Case Study - A tale of two Nonprofits

A tale of two Nonprofits

By now it should seem obvious or at least a good idea to have an ERM process in place and to reevaluate it regularly to account for changes in your risk environment. Some organizations will immediately see the need to put a program in place, others will put it off until they have more time. There will never be a good time to put an ERM program in place. There is only now. The very nature of risk and especially significant risk is that to a large degree, it will always be unpredictable.

Let's talk about two nonprofits that considered implementing an ERM program. One took the position that it was a good idea, but could not find the time to do the work. The other decided to "do it now".

Both organizations had some similarities. Both had been in business for over 30 years, both had long term Executive Directors and strong boards, both provided service to their community through volunteers, both existed through a combination of individual donations and grants, but from different organizations, and as you might expect for organizations that had existed over that many years, both had to deal with unexpected events that caused plans and objectives to be constrained or delayed.

The first organization had a "we'll handle it" approach to dealing with unexpected adverse situations. As these events occurred, the management team and the board would come together, assess the severity of the situation, and either revise current plans, cut programs or staff or find some way to handle the situation. In most cases, the event was overcome. New staff were hired to replace unexpected turnover, or new sources of funds identified and programs either continued as they had, or in their revised form and the organization went on.

But each time these events occurred, the management team and the board had to alter their focus to deal with the situation at hand and in some cases, lost their focus on other goals and objectives. As a result, there were almost always unintended consequences that affected other parts of the organization because the resolution to the immediate crisis was not always aligned with strategic plans, which caused the organization to make subsequent adjustments to other programs or personnel to compensate for the unintended consequences of the resolution to the crisis. In other words, solutions were usually quick fixes that had the potential to cause other problems as opposed to a well thought out more comprehensive course of action.

When the Executive Director was asked to consider implementing a formal ERM process, the ED said that it seemed like a good idea, but they had survived for this long without one that and despite the fact that each crisis consumed a significant amount of time on the part of the board, management, management and staff, they really did not have to time to put such a program in place.

The second organization took a different approach.

The organization had been in existence for 30 years without experiencing significant setbacks due to unforeseen risks. Risk events were being handled as required, but as with the first organization, not without an impact on programs and staff. But even though risk was being managed, they also recognized there was a growing trend towards greater program accountability through the measurement of outcomes and benchmarking. GuideStar and other nonprofit rating agencies were increasingly being utilized to bolster donor confidence and it was important for the organization to maintain or achieve satisfactory ratings. They had recently developed a 5-year strategic plan and the development of an ERM program. To coincide with that plan seemed to make sense.

As a result, the Executive Director decided to undertake the initiative to develop a more formal ERM program and proceeded with the full support of the board. The process they took will be described below. In all it took about 40 hours of time for each of six individuals involved in the process (three board members, the ED and two staff) and three months of elapsed time to complete the project. There were a number of risks identified with varying levels of impact with two surfacing as significant. A plan to deal with the two most significant risks was developed shortly after completing the ERM program, with the others to be dealt with over time, but with specific target dates for completion.

It was shortly after that the worst case scenario and one of the two most significant risks occurred the organization unexpectedly lost their Executive Director.

It was something that was unimaginable during the time that the ERM program was being developed, but the organization developed a thorough plan for how to deal with such a scenario none-the-less.

In short, the succession plan that was developed as a part of the ERM program was put into action, a new Executive Director put in place and aside from what you might expect as normal transition issues, the organization continued on with their mission without any significant impact on their mission, staff or clients.

The first organization had also recently developed a 3-5 year strategic plan. As part of the development of that plan, they had of course undertaken a SWOT (Strengths, Weaknesses, Opportunities and Threats) analysis and decided that since the SWOT considered both weaknesses and threats the undertaking a separate ERM initiative was not necessary. As described earlier, however, ERM does not only evaluate weakness and threats, it also evaluates risks to the organization's strengths and opportunities. As with the second organization, the ED was considered a significant strength.

As with the second organization, they too unexpectedly lost their Executive Director. Their transition was not as seamless as was the case with the second organization.

Since both organizations had long term EDs, much of the organizational knowledge was stored in the EDs head. Simple things like normal day-to-day processes and routines, personal contacts and even potential grant opportunities, and organizational history were matters that neither ED took or had the time to share with other members of the organization including the assistant director.

Where the second organization recognized this as a risk that needed to be dealt with, the first organization simply considered that experience to be one of the EDs strengths. The risk of suddenly losing that experience not something that was discussed.

In the second organization's development of a succession

plan for the ED, not only was consideration given to the person who succeed the ED, but also time was taken to document and share the ED's 30 years of knowledge with the assistance director and members of the staff.

The first organization even had a difficult time accessing the EDs email and personal records. Grant opportunities the ED was pursuing were nearly missed. In addition, the sudden heavy burden of on the assistant director having to fill in for the ED while still having to perform all the tasks of the assistant's job nearly caused the organization to lose that person too.

The good news, both organizations survived the crisis and continue to prosper. However, while the mission, goals and objective of the second organization continued without missing a beat, the first organization had a significant delay in the process of executing their plans. There is no way to know what may have been lost in that protracted transition in terms of client service, donor support or in staff morale.

Which organization would you like to be?

Chapter 13

Conclusion

In conclusion, managing risk is a choice. It is not a process that is mandated or required by anyone. You can choose to formally manage it as we have described in this book, manage it on and ad hoc bases or not manage it at all and simply deal with each crisis as it occurs.

In our view, it is far better to be proactive than reactive. It is better to know a risk can occur even if there is little that can be done to avoid the risk than to have it catch you by surprise.

Managing your risk should not be something that constrains your organization or inhibits your ability to accomplish goals. On the contrary, it should provide you with a higher degree of confidence that you will be able to accomplish your goals and objectives. It should be a way of clearing your path to success or a way to alter your course to avoid failure.

From our point of view, the choice is simple. Managing risk is no different than having a business plan or process that guides your organization to success. It is simply a plan for the unexpected and a process to minimize the uncertainty all organizations face.

So How Do I Begin?

Start the ERM process by identifying how your risks relate to strategy, goals and objectives. Recording your risks can be as simple as documenting your risk in a WORD document to developing various spreadsheets (samples can be found in the appendices) and to help evaluate and score your risk. The important thing is to make sure your thoughts are written down somewhere so they can be periodically reviewed, updated, explained to others for example your Board of Directors.

What goals and objectives are "must do" items? What absolutely needs to be accomplished in order to achieve your mission this year? With multiple objectives, it may be hard to choose, but identify the one or two objectives that are so crucial that your organization will fail if they are not accomplished. If you can't decide, pick one or two to begin with. A sound ERM program is something that is built over time, not something you "finish" in one sitting.

What you will do with this the selection is to determine or identify the risks that will affect it. What risks exist that will cause that objective to fail. The process that follows will take you through the steps necessary to identify and deal with the specific risks related to that one objective. Once you go through the process for that first objective, you simply repeat the process, as time allows, for the balance of your goals and objectives. Over time, you will have built a program that addresses all your objectives, and one that deals with the risks that affect them.

To identify the risks, a good brainstorming session can be useful. Prepare a pre-list of all the things that you can think of that could go wrong. Refine the list as a team. Involve as many people within the organization as practical so that there is representation from a broad cross section of the functions of the organization. Bring in some outside individuals, as appropriate, for example, board members, major donors, or anyone that you believe has enough knowledge and interest in the organization to want it to succeed.

The first pass at building such a list will yield a hodgepodge of thoughts and ideas, some of which may be trivial, but many of which will be very important. Take that loose collection of thoughts, group them by kind and begin to build risk categories.

A set of 10-12 categories is commonly used. You can have more or less, but too many or too few will limit your ability to effectively deal with those risks. A sample of risk categories can be found in Appendix 2. As with the ERM process as a whole, this document now becomes a continuous work-in-progress. Something that you will periodically review, update and use in the overall evaluation of your risk.

Now hold that list of risk categories up against those one or two most important goals or objectives.

Which of the risk categories will have an impact on that objective? Not every risk you've considered in the development of those categories will affect every goal or objective, but the list will help ensure that you've considered most of your risks. What is the specific risk within any given category that is likely to have an impact on that goal? What will the effect be?

It is certainly possible that major goals and objectives could be affected by all of the 10-12 categories of risk that were previously identified. But more likely it will be some subset of the full set.

Now rank each of the risks within that subset. Using a scale of 1-5 (5 being high) as described above, how likely is that risk going to occur? If it occurs, using the same scale of 1-5, how significant will the impact be?

The ranking should fall out quite easily, allowing you to see those risks that are most likely to occur, that will have the greatest impact to that goal or objective.

By going through the process in this manner, you will identify only those risks that are most significant to that specific goal. Yes, at some point you will need to address all of your risks, but that will be accomplished as you build your ERM program over time. For the moment, all you need to deal with are the risks that will affect that one goal.

Now you can work on how to mitigate that risk. What can be done to reduce the likelihood of that risk occurring or the impact it will have? What is your plan?

Take each goal and objective and each risk one at a time. Trying to address every risk all at once might be too overwhelming.

Your plan will build over time and you will be able to deal with more of your risks as the process continues. You'll be taking control of the elements in your environment that can limit your success.

At the end of the day, if your organization is prey to a significant risk that greatly impacts it, you want to be able to know and attest that you have taken all reasonable steps to manage risk.

Appendix 1

Sample Enterprise Risk Management Context and Rationale

External Context

Our organization enjoys an external environment in which it provides a unique service offering with little or no competition along with a good reputation. There are a large number of clients in the area allowing for significant growth potential. And there is a large pool of experienced volunteers available to serve the existing and potential client base. The organization has a dedicated Executive Director and staff and has been in existence for 30 years without experiencing significant setbacks due to unforeseen risks. There is also a trend towards greater program accountability through the measurement of outcomes and benchmarking. GuideStar and other nonprofit rating agencies are increasingly being utilized, making the organization more valuable in helping the client community maintain or achieve satisfactory ratings. It also exists in an environment where the National brand has little benefit or risk for the organization. Within the external environment however, the organization needs to continually be aware of the risks that could impact its continued success.

These may include:

- The health of the economy, good or bad, that may impact the funding or existence of clients resulting in a loss of engagements and revenue;

- Changes in tax structure that could affect both clients and the organization itself;

- DOL (Dept. of Labor) changes in how employees are categorized as exempt or non-exempt potentially increasing the cost structure of our client companies and the organization itself as more staff could be subject to overtime rules. These changes could result in less money available for the organization's engagements as well as increasing costs to the annual budget.

The organization also needs to:

- Maintain its brand strength within the known community; and

- Be cognizant of the quality of their life/service balance

Internal Context

The organization has a well-defined and well-established set of core values upon which it can base its work and its treatment of the highly knowledgeable, capable and dedicated team of staff and volunteers. It has a very supportive Board that understands and is committed to the governance and leadership process and pipeline, which has been actively engaged, dedicated and passionate about its mission for the past 30 years. This strong internal environment should allow the organization to continue in its success.

Within this internal environment, however the organization

needs to remember that volunteers are stakeholders/clients as well and need to have a meaningful experience through their service. Due to normal attrition of staff and volunteers, there needs to be a smooth transfer of knowledge from staff to volunteers and from volunteers to volunteers to ensure the high quality of service is maintained over time.

The organization has adopted a 3 year rolling strategic plan model. This allows them to clarify their vision & plan annually and ensures that at any point in time, they will always have a 3 year strategic plan.

Rationale

Currently, there is no formal risk management process in place. This is not to say that risks are not being managed, but a formal risk management process will help ensure that risks are addressed and managed on a continual basis to consider changes to the context of the risks as described above.

Appendix 2

Example Risk Category Descriptions

Business Process

- Established office process not being followed by both volunteers and staff
  - › The risk is that lack of adherence may cause the limited staff extra work resulting in operational inefficiencies and the inability to complete their entire workload.

- Staff size and lack of co-location
  - › The limited number of staff and the fact that they work different hours from physically separate locations may constrain both volunteers and other staff members from gaining access to information.
  - › This may also have a direct impact with staff who are getting bogged down in the weeds due to taking on job tasks of others.

Human Resources

- Succession planning

  › The risk of not having the ability to rapidly replace staff members as the occasions occur.

- Size

  › The limited size of the staff may put the number tasks staff is able to handle at any given time at risk.

- Cerebral Information Storage (keeping information in one head)

  › The risk that information about processes, clients or other relationships are kept in individual heads not documented or easily transferrable to other or new staff. This presents a risk to both enable filling in for unavailable staff or knowledge transfer if a staff member leaves.

Information Technology

- Security Protocols (risk is compromising sensitive client data)

  › Confidential client information may be on personal laptops (donor lists, financial records, etc.) and said laptop may not be password protected – what happens if it is stolen? Further, what is the legal liability?

- Remote Access Technology (risk is that the system presently used is resulting in operating inefficiencies)

  › The number of people who can be on simultaneously from a remote location is very limited

  › The speed of the actual remote access does not

keep up with the work speed of the individual using it which can result in significant frustration.

Reputational

- The risk of existing client loss or new client gain due to client perception of:

  › Engagement quality, timeliness & resultant outcomes

  › Volunteers quality & timeliness

Sales and marketing

- The risk to revenue loss due to:

  › Competition

  › Staff size limitations

  › Lack of brand awareness

Governance

- The risk is that there would be inadequate governance which is impacted by:

  › The level of Board engagement

  › Cultivation and openness of Board members to a diversity of perspective

  › Leadership is trained in the manner we recommend to our clients

  › Adequacy of succession planning

Financial

- The risks to financial solvency are:

  › Changes to corporate of government funding programs who provide sponsorships

  › Changes to DOL (Department of Labor) rules

regarding classification of employees as exempt/
non-exempt could increase payroll cost.

› Changes to key donor/sponsors financial
situation that could impact their philanthropy.

Appendix 3

Sample Likelihood and Impact Scales

Likelihood and Impact Scales					
Likelihood Score		General	Timeframe	Frequency	Intensity
5		Definitely	Immediately	Very Often	At its highest
4		More Than	3 Months	Often	Very high
3		Normally	12 Months	Periodically	Increasing
2		Sometimes	30 Months	Occasionally	Normal
1		Rarely	60 Months	Rarely	Low
Impact Score		Revenue	Donor Loss	Grant Loss	Staff Loss
5		100%	>25	50%	4
4		75%	15-24	25%	3
3		50%	10-14	10%	2
2		25%	5-9	5%	1
1		<10%	<5	<5%	0

Appendix 4

Sample ERM Manual

Sample Enterprise
Risk Manual

The following is an example of a risk manual for ERM. The manual should include all relevant risks that have been identified and how they relate to important goals and objectives of the organization. It should also include an analysis of how likely the risk is to occur and the severity of the impact or consequence. Most important is the mitigation steps being taken to reduce the likelihood and/or impact. The purpose is this manual is to provide a central point of documentation on risks that may be periodically reviewed, updated or otherwise use to help minimize obstacles that could inhibit the forward movement of the organization. The sample only list one or two examples of a risk. A full manual should be a working document that includes all risks. It should also be a document that builds over time.

Table of Contents

Enterprise Risk Management Context and Rationale

External Context

The organization has a dedicated Executive Director and staff and has been in existence for 30 years without experiencing significant setbacks due to unforeseen risks. There is also a trend towards greater program accountability through the measurement of outcomes and benchmarking.

Within the external environment the organization needs to continually be aware of the risks that could impact its continued success.

These may include:

- The health of the economy, good or bad, that may impact funding;

- Changes in tax structure that could affect the organization;

- Brand strength within the known community; and

- The quality of their service.

Internal Context

The organization has a well-defined and well-established set of core values upon which it can base its work and its treatment of the highly knowledgeable, capable and dedicated team of staff and volunteers. It has a very supportive Board that understands and is committed to the governance and leadership process and pipeline, which has been actively engaged, dedicated and passionate about its mission for the past 30 years. This strong internal environment should allow the organization to continue in its success.

Rationale

While there is no immediate concern with respect to risk in the internal and external environment, there is no formal risk management process in place. This is not to say that risks are not being managed, but a formal risk management process will help ensure that risks are addressed and managed on a continual basis to consider changes to the context of the risks as described above.

Likelihood and Impact Scales

All risks should be viewed consistently across the organization. This helps ensure that the magnitude of any one risk can be reasonably compared to that of another. This helps to determine priorities, and the extent of mitigation process that will be applied to any given risk in order to address the most significant risks in the most cost effective manner.

The following scales are used in the evaluation of risks:

Likelihood and Impact Scales

Likelihood Score	General	Timeframe	Frequency	Intensity
5	Definitely	Immediately	Very Often	At its highest
4	More Than	3 Months	Often	Very high
3	Normally	12 Months	Periodically	Increasing
2	Sometimes	30 Months	Occasionally	Normal
1	Rarely	60 Months	Rarely	Low

Impact Score	Revenue	Donor Loss	Grant Loss	Staff Loss
5	100%	>25	50%	4
4	75%	15-24	25%	3
3	50%	10-14	10%	2
2	25%	5-9	5%	1
1	<10%	<5	<5%	0

* Note: The purpose of four categories of likelihood is to allow some level of discretion in the evaluation of the likelihood of various risks may occur. For example, a new regulation may be on the horizon, but will not occur within the next 30 months. Therefore, that risk is subject to the Timeframe scale. Competition is ever present, but may be at its lowest level at the point of time the risk was considered. Therefore, competitive risk more easily determined based on Intensity as opposed to Timeframe. The Frequency category may more easily be applied to specific reoccurring events, such as errors. The General category may apply to risks that are intuitively obvious.

Risk Categories and descriptions

The following are summaries of risks that should be considered. The nature of this risk may change from time to time and should be reevaluated periodically.

Business Process

❖ Established office process not being followed by both volunteers and staff.

o The risk is that lack of adherence may cause the limited staff extra work resulting in operational inefficiencies and the inability to complete their entire workload.

HR - Staff

❖ Succession planning

○ The risk of not having the ability to rapidly replace staff members as the occasions occur.

❖ Size

○ The limited size of the staff may limit the number of tasks staff is able to handle at any given time at risk.

❖ Information kept in key staff members head

○ The risk that information about processes or relationships is in individual heads not documented or easily transferrable to other or new staff. This presents a risk to both enable filling in for unavailable staff or knowledge transfer if a staff member leaves.

Reputational

❖ The risk of existing donor loss or new donor gain due to poor perception of the organization

Governance

❖ The risk is that there would be inadequate governance which is impacted by:

○ The level of Board engagement.

○ Lack of leadership training

○ Adequacy of succession planning.

Strategies and Associated Risk: Services

Our Services will address what the market needs as expressed by clients, funders, and other stakeholders.

Significant Risks

The following risks are likely to affect the outcome of this strategy Objective:

Risk Category	Risk Issue
HR - Staff	Cerebral Information Storage
Reputational	Service quality
HR - Staff	Succession planning

Risk Mitigation

The following actions are being taken to mitigate these risks:

HR Staff: Succession Planning

The risk of not having the ability to rapidly replace staff members as the occasions occur.

Mitigation Process
• Documenting major processes
• Cross-training where appropriate, such as Dropbox, SurveyMonkey and QuickBooks

Reputational: Service quality

The risk of existing client loss or new client gain due to client perception of: Volunteers quality & timelines

Mitigation Process
• Implementing extensive new staff and volunteer training
• Offering quarterly meetings/training to all staff and volunteers

Appendix 5

ERM Survey

Protiviti has conducted the same survey with North Carolina State University's ERM Initiative for several years. The following question was answered by public companies, privately held companies and not-for-profit organizations. Here is the question and the answer.

Overall, what is your impression of the magnitude and severity of risks your organization will be facing with respect to reaching or exceeding profitability, (or funding) targets over the next 12 months?	2018	2017	2016
Not-for-profits	5.5	5.8	5.7

1=Extremely Low and 10=Extensive

Public companies rated this a 6.1 in 2018. This begs the question whether or nonprofits are looking at the world through too rosy a filter. It is up to Boards of these organizations to be sure that a sense of awareness and realism about risk is practiced among themselves and the staff and volunteers of the organization.

Source: "Executive Perspectives on Top Risks for 2018" by Protiviti and NCSU ERM Initiative, p.56

Appendix 6

Funding risks by type of funder

All of these risks can be exacerbated by rising expenses due to inflation or greater demands on an organization.

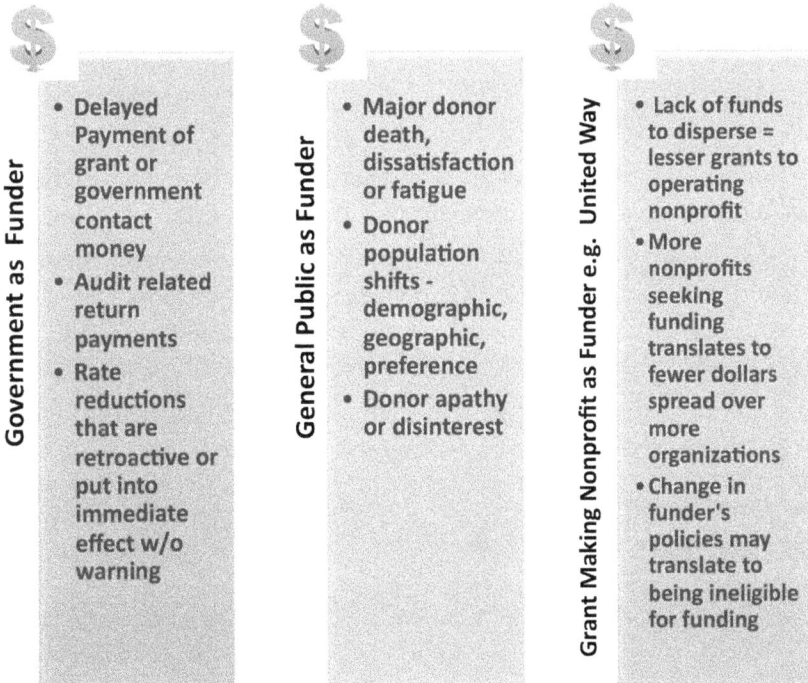

Government as Funder
- Delayed Payment of grant or government contact money
- Audit related return payments
- Rate reductions that are retroactive or put into immediate effect w/o warning

General Public as Funder
- Major donor death, dissatisfaction or fatigue
- Donor population shifts - demographic, geographic, preference
- Donor apathy or disinterest

Grant Making Nonprofit as Funder e.g. United Way
- Lack of funds to disperse = lesser grants to operating nonprofit
- More nonprofits seeking funding translates to fewer dollars spread over more organizations
- Change in funder's policies may translate to being ineligible for funding

Appendix 7

Funding Shortfall Mitigation Plan Examples

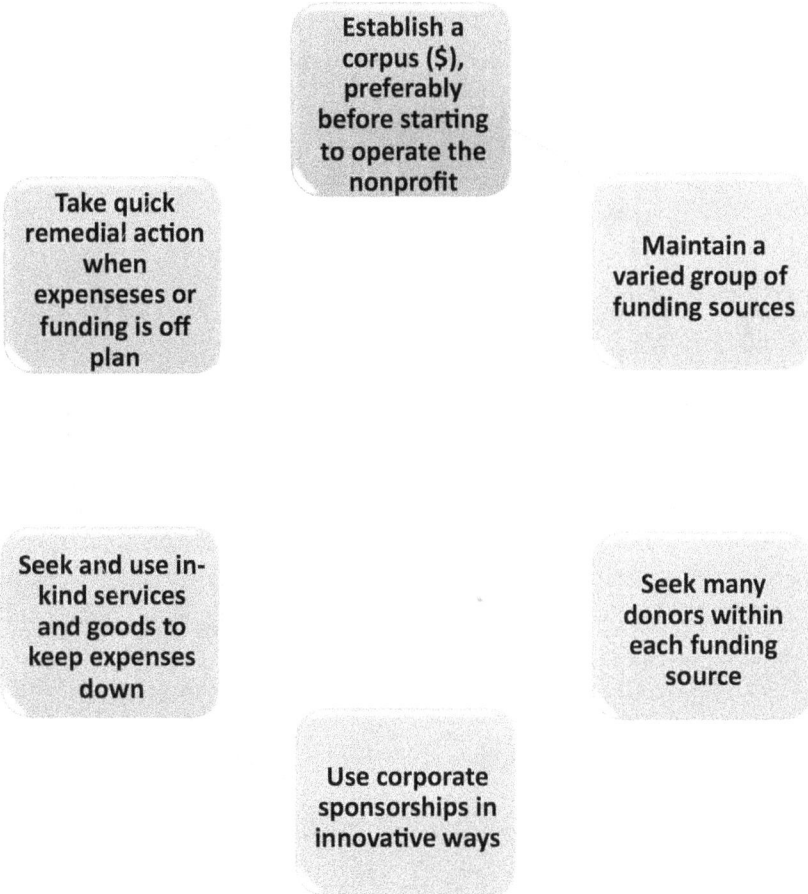

Establish a corpus ($), preferably before starting to operate the nonprofit

Take quick remedial action when expenseses or funding is off plan

Maintain a varied group of funding sources

Seek and use in-kind services and goods to keep expenses down

Seek many donors within each funding source

Use corporate sponsorships in innovative ways

Appendix 8

Keeping Insurance Costs Down

The Building Blocks of Keeping Insurance Costs Down

Take as large a deductible as prudent	Negotiate for added value service from agent/broker	Make sure policy limits are sufficient but not higher than needed
Rent vs Own Property In Many Markets	Avoid organization owned vehicles as much as possible	Get quotes from other insurers every couple of years
Show agent/carrier all the safety and risk management practices in place	Maintain safety and risk management practices to reduce claims and build a good claims history	Comply with all the policy requirements , e.g. how and when to report claims

Notes by Chapter

Chapter 1

1. "Triangle YWCA closes after 110 years" WRAL New. February 29, 2012, http://www.wral.com/news/local/story/10794946/

2. "Aspen Film Festival Nonprofit Sued by Fired Executive Director" by Michael Wyland, Aspen Daily News. May 19, 2017

3. "Sources: Huntsman Cancer Institute director to be reinstated Tuesday" by Daphne Chen and Ben Lockhart, Deseret News. April 24, 2017 http://www.deseretnews.com/article/865678531/Soures-Huntsman-Cancer-Institute-director-to-be-reinstated-Tuesday.html

4. "Oklahoma Nonprofit Responds to Former US Congressman Suit," The Associated Press. May 31, 2017

5. "United Way, Faced With Fewer Donors, Is Giving Away Less" by David Cay Johnston, The New York Times. November 9, 1997, http://www.nytimes.com/1997/11/09/us/united-way-faced-with-fewer-donors-is-giving-away-less.html

6. https://www.forbes.com/companies/united-way-worldwide/

7. "Orange Nonprofit Will Pay 1.7 Million to Settle Charges of Falsifying Records" by Adam Elmharek and Thy Vo, Voice of OC., March 15, 2015, http://voiceofoc.org/2015/03/garden-grove-nonprofit-fined-1-7-million-for-falsifying-records/

8. "Goodwill fined more than $100K after worker's gruesome death" by Marjie Lundstrom, Sacramento Bee. April 8, 2017, http://www.sacbee.com/news/investigations/the-public-eye/article143481114.html

Chapter 2

1. https://www.economist.com/finance-and-economics/2018/02/15/recent-tax-reforms-in-america-will-hurt-charities

Chapter 3

1. "Independent Adoption Center Collapse Was Abrupt, But Not Without Warning Signs" by John Kelly, Chronicle of Social Change. February 6, 2017, https://chronicleofsocialchange.org/

Chapter 5

1. http://www.marchofdimes.org/mission/a-history-of-the-march-of-dimes.aspx "A history of the March of Dimes"

Chapter 7

1. Michael Mauboussin on Strategy. March 20, 2007 "Explaining the Wisdom of the Crowds" Legg Mason Capital Management

2. Ibid.

Chapter 10

1. news@insurancejournal.com Insurance Headlines "Insurers Off The Hook For West Virginia Hole-In-One Tournament Payouts" December 29, 2017